One Percenter

One Percenter

The Legend of
THE OUTLAW BIKER

Dave Nichols

MOTORBOOKS

First published in 2007 by Motorbooks, an imprint of MBI Publishing Company, Galtier Plaza, Suite 200, 380 Jackson Street, St. Paul, MN 55101 USA

MBI Publishing Company titles are also available at discounts in bulk quantity for industrial or sales-promotional use. For details write to Special Sales Manager at MBI Publishing Company, Galtier Plaza, Suite 200, 380 Jackson Street, St. Paul, MN 55101 USA

To find out more about our books, join us online at www.motorbooks.com.

Library of Congress Cataloging-in-Publication Data

Nichols, Dave, 1954–
  One percenter : the legend of the outlaw biker / by Dave Nichols.
    p. cm.
  ISBN: 978-0-7603-2998-6 (hardbound w/ jacket)
  1. Motorcycle gangs—United States. 2. Motorcycle clubs—United States—History. 3. Motorcycling—United States,—History. I. Title.

HV6439.U5N53 2007
364.106'60973—dc22

                              2007024642

Editor: Darwin Holmstrom
Designer: Tom Heffron

Printed in the USA

Interior Photography: Kim Peterson
Cover Photograph: copyright 2007 Michael Lichter

CONTENTS

INTRODUCTION

Motorcycle Mavericks

It is not a coincidence that you are holding this book in your hands. The fact that you are drawn to this subject means that there is a bit of the rebel in you. You have a mischievous streak and you don't fit in with the bland suits out there waiting in line for Starbuck's non-fat lattes. You have an artistic spark and an intelligence that pushes the edges of the reality that you've been handed. You will not simply accept conformity; there's a bit of the outsider in you. You question authority. Naturally, this means that you don't fit in with "the program." You have little patience with the status quo and enjoy shaking things up a bit. I know you because I don't fit into society's mold either. We are rebels, you and I, and we are about to embark on a fascinating adventure.

We are about to set sail beyond the edge of the world, beyond the drawn boundaries of convention, to world's end and back, and where we are going there be dragons. We are about to become anthropologists of the modern age, looking for the origin of an ancient tribe whose name is Rebellion. We will go spelunking in forgotten caves of consciousness where the darkness has a life of its own. To explore the history of motorcycles' rebels is to examine the history of the rebel spirit itself. We will look back in time to uncover the source of our discontent.

The modern outlaw biker is linked in spirit to ancient tribes of radical thinkers, people who would not go quietly into the night, but raged with the dazzling fire of nonconformity and lived outside the box. Thus, we will unearth the seeds of rebellion sown by the Vikings, the Huns, the Mongols, the mercenary knights, and the pirates of old. Within the tattered pages of their history we will find the birthplace of the outlaw biker. We will examine clues left by those who dared to cross perilous seas in search of a free nation in America. We will recognize our own rebel yell.

In the new world of America the seeds of rebellion blossomed into the new forms of the frontiersman, the mountain man, the cowboy, and the Old West outlaw. These earlier American rebels gave birth to the outlaw biker, a demon spawned when returning servicemen from World War II tried to calm their savage inner beasts by twisting the throttles of powerful motorcycles and letting that V-twin roar become their new collective voice.

The road from outcast to outlaw often turns out to be a short trip. Many war-ravaged veterans returned home to an America that did not want to deal with them. War is always nasty business, and the Disneyesque, homogenized, seemingly safe facade of America did not know what to do when faced with the bloody fangs of its own creation. When Johnny came marching home, he wasn't the same sweet boy who trotted off to war like a good puppy. Once you learn to kill and think on your feet in order to survive, you just don't fit into the same little box anymore.

We will see how "drinking clubs with motorcycle problems" evolved in the public mind into vicious outlaw gangs and how the media fostered this frightening image. We will also delve into how marketing and media brought the outlaw image to the masses, how the film *Easy Rider* ignited an entire generation in search of a celluloid anthem and how the motorcycle magazine *Easyriders* gave the biker lifestyle its own tongue.

Just as all things in nature run their course, so we will see how history closes its chapters on bygone rebels. We'll examine how the edges of the world closed in to halt the pillage of the Vikings; how the seas grew smaller to end the golden age of pirates; how the Wild West was tamed to end the days of the cowboy and the gunslinger. In every case, the broad map of reality was drawn in to limit the spread of nonconformity. Once limitless frontiers close their borders, civilization reins in lawlessness.

So many times we have found our most frightening bad boys have become the darlings of the media in watered down, romantic versions of themselves, from dime-store novels of Billy the Kid to comic books of Blackbeard. The media has made modern mavericks such as Billy Lane and

There's an old saying: "Ladies love outlaws." Any biker will tell you that saying is true.

The road from outcast to first class has been a long one for the one percenter.

Jesse James into TV sensations, seen from the safe side of the cathode-ray television tube, like tigers behind glass.

We will look at the homogenization of the outlaw biker image in an age when motorcycle jackets became a fashion statement and the Harley-Davidson Motor Company markets sanitized rebellion to the masses. The rise of the RUBBIE (rich urban biker) will be examined as Americans from all walks of life discovered the freedom found on two wheels. Today, the scary-looking biker who roars up next to you at a stoplight might very well be your doctor or lawyer converted to weekend warrior.

We will witness the rise and fall of the one percenter culture, from wild one to mild one. Yet in every age, society, and culture there is a need for the nonconformist. Without the heady, blazing fire of rebellion, there is no one to stir the cauldron of convention or keep rational society on its toes. In all great myths and stories from all times and lands, there has always been "the one" who has come forward to shake things up, to create change. Indeed, it is the bad boy, the rebel in society, who helps to define the lines and charts of society's course. The outlaw dares to travel beyond the safety of the map of the known world and push until something pushes back. That is our job, for you and I are rebels in a time that needs us badly.

Aye, we are venturing off the map . . . there be dragons here.

CHAPTER 1

The Seeds of Rebellion

WHEREIN WE WILL LOOK AT A BRIEF HISTORY OF THOSE
WHO TURNED AWAY FROM SOCIETY AND CONVENTION IN
FAVOR OF FREEDOM: THE MERCENARY KNIGHTS,
MONGOLS, VIKINGS, HUNS, AND PIRATES. ALL WERE
FORERUNNERS TO THE MODERN OUTLAW BIKER.

It has been said that bikers are born bikers, not made into bikers. Rebellion is often the result of not fitting in with others. Children can be some of the cruelest people on earth. If a playmate doesn't fit in because he or she is too tall or too short, too fat or too skinny, has crooked teeth or big ears, or any number of perceived differences, children can be downright brutal in their ability to bully or abuse.

I didn't fit in during my school years because I had no interest in sports whatsoever. I didn't fit into any of the usual school cliques: I wasn't a social climber or a fashion trendsetter. I wasn't in the chess club or computer club. Sports just seemed like a waste of time to me. But motorcycles . . . they were something different. I loved motorcycles and rushed out to get my learner's permit at the tender age of 15. In Florida, where I grew up, you could ride a small motorcycle under a certain brake horsepower at that age.

I had watched every episode of NBC's *Then Came Bronson* TV series in 1969 and was drawn to the character of laconic drifter Jim Bronson, as played by Michael Parks. I was also drawn to the little red Harley-Davidson Sportster that transported him to each new adventure. The bike was the conveyance of choice for this free spirit. He would ride into a small town every week, get a job and make a few bucks to buy beef jerky and gasoline, which was apparently all a gypsy biker needed on the road to adventure.

Most memorable was the show's opening, in which we would see Bronson pull up to a red light next to a family station wagon. The weary, work-worn driver of the wagon would look longingly at Bronson's Sportster before asking, "Where you headed?"

"Wherever I end up, I guess," was Bronson's reply.

"Man," the straight citizen would lament, "I sure wish I were you."

"Well," Bronson would grin before roaring off, "Hang in there."

Yeah, hang in there you poor son-of-a-bitch. I knew right then and there which of those two guys I wanted to be and it sure as hell wasn't the poor slob in the rusty station wagon, with a clock to punch and a mortgage to pay. And I wasn't alone. The summer after *Then Came Bronson* debuted, more people went out and bought street bikes than in any summer before. Harley-Davidson picked up on this trend and even came out with a special Sportster in Bronson Red.

Also in the summer of 1969, the film *Easy Rider* premiered in theaters all across America. I had to beg my parents to take me to the film because of its R rating. I'll never forget how embarrassed I was to have my timid mother sit through that movie with its nudity, foul language, and drug use. I thought I was going to crawl under the sticky theater seat when John Kay of Steppenwolf began screaming "God Damn the Pusher" over and over again. My face still gets red when I remember that moment. Yet I came out of the movie house a convert to the two-wheeled lifestyle. I wanted a chopper. I wanted to put on a leather jacket and roar across the country, flipping off the squares and laughing at the uptight society that raised me. I wanted to *be* Peter Fonda because, to me, he was the embodiment of cool.

During one of the druggy campfire scenes in the film, Peter Fonda takes a toke of marijuana and asks Luke Askew and Dennis Hopper, "Have you ever wanted to be anyone else?"

Luke Askew squints in the pot smoke and slurs, "I'd like to try Porky Pig."

Hopper giggles and Fonda just nods. "I never wanted to be anybody else." Well, of course you never wanted to be anybody else; you're Captain America, you're Peter friggin' Fonda, the standard by which all coolness is measured. In that moment, my friends, the die was cast and the rebel in me found a voice. Without ever having thrown my leg over a motorcycle I knew

In 1969, the film Easy Rider *made many a young man run out and buy a nasty murdercycle.*

that there was something about riding one that had to do with freedom, with the feeling of the wind in your hair and bugs in your teeth. By whatever name that feeling went, I wanted it.

As it turns out, I was right. Few things I've found in life give me the same sense of freedom I feel while blasting down the road on a motorcycle, especially if it's a custom chopper.

What makes one child a quiet computer geek and another a football hero? What makes a kid a rebel? It's been said that you can tell which kid is going to grow up to be a social outcast just by watching them in kindergarten. Are bikers born with the need to turn up their collars and sit in the corner of the classroom, listening for the sound of a Harley passing by? Someone once told me that the biker-to-be is the kid who won't just follow along and take orders. He won't be bullied either. He is the kid who pushes back—he might not win every fight but he won't put up with any crap. The rebel apparently has a very low tolerance for bullshit of any kind. The lone wolf listens to the tune of a different drummer all right; it's the thump of a big V-twin motor that gets his pulse pounding.

How far back would we have to go to trace our rebel roots? Could the origin of rebellion and search for personal freedom go all the way back to the cave dweller? Imagine a tribe of Neanderthals huddled in their cave, gnawing on the bones of some slow moving mammal, hoping that they can figure out that "fire thing" pretty soon because sushi might work for fish, but raw badger sucks! The cave women are squashing some kind of berries into a paste, a couple of the men are arguing over the score of the sloth toss regionals, and several furry kids are having a contest to see who can land on their heads hardest and live.

Out in front of the cave squats Zog, carving the first wheel out of stone. He sips a strange brew of hops and water from a gourd and gazes across the valley toward the setting sun. You just know he's thinking, "If I can carve another one of these round things, I'm gonna ride the hell away from these losers."

Let's leave Zog with his thoughts (mainly because there's no way to prove that the first rebel outlaw was a caveman) and take a look at the history of those who turned away from society and convention to forge their own path. Who were the forerunners of the outlaw biker? There is no doubt that there have been select tribes throughout history that have left their bloody marks on the human psyche, scars that are still borne by the outlaw bikers of our time. The outlaw biker subculture borrows many elements of its lifestyle from ancient warriors of many lands and times. Ever notice that

The feel of riding a custom chopper down the road is right up there with sex.

Flying free with the wind in their hair, modern day outlaws are the Vikings of the road.

biker tattoos include images of savage Vikings, Celtic weaves, or piratical skull and crossbones? Well, there's a reason for this. You see, one percenters provide vessels through which the warrior outlaw spirit lives today. They are among the few remaining tribes that still embody the spirit of freedom.

To understand how and why one percenters embody this long outlaw tradition, we need to look at a few of the more notorious savage tribes that have embodied the outlaw spirit throughout history. It is no accident that many motorcycle clubs have taken their names from such tribes. Two such historical one percenter clubs are the Huns and the Mongols. We will begin our journey back in time with an overview of these marauding clans of horsemen: the original Wild Ones.

THE HUNS

Historians tell us that the Huns came from the East to besiege the Roman Empire in the late fourth century A.D. and quickly conquered most of Europe. The Huns true origin is unknown, but we do know that they were among the nomadic tribes of the Asian steppes. They were present in the most ancient times in Mesopotamia and have even been linked with the Israelites in different times throughout history. The very name Hun conjures up wild images of nomadic barbarians on horseback, proud warriors and free spirits. But these ancient people were far more complex than most of us realize.

The Huns' origin may stretch back to earlier peoples of the ancient Middle East: the Sumerians and the Scythians. Researchers discovered this potential link by comparing modern Hungarian (Magyar) and other related languages with documents of the ancient Middle East. Linguistic similarities suggested a possible common origin.

The territories of the Huns at various times stretched from Central Asia to Central Europe, from Siberia and China to North India. To consider them as simply barbaric nomads casts aside their amazing history. The Huns' villages had paved streets, stone buildings, agriculture and metallurgy, and the Huns had a written language. Chinese historians distinguish between Mongols and Huns, stating that the earlier Huns were much more advanced than the Mongol tribes that came after them.

The Huns were a complex group of different tribes and peoples rather than a single nation. After their arrival in Europe, the Hun tribes developed their own identity. Some established themselves as an organized state; others

Iron horsemen on metal steeds conjure up images of the Huns of old.

were assimilated by non-related nations. Their heritage has been transferred to many Eurasian peoples, including the Uyghurs of Western China and several Turkish and Ugro-Finnic tribes. Two of these tribes have given their name to modern European states: the Bulgars and the Magyars.

Some believe that there is a direct connection between Attila the Hun and the Hungarian kings. The legendary Attila the Hun (405–453), also known as Attila the Scourge of God, was the Huns' most powerful king. He reigned over what was, at the time, Europe's largest empire from 434 until his death. His empire stretched from Germany and the Netherlands to the Ural River in Russia, and from the Danube River to Poland and Estonia. During his rule, he was one of the Roman Empire's greatest enemies.

Equally legendary were his fierce battles. Attila invaded the Balkans twice and encircled Constantinople in his second invasion. He marched through France as far as Orléans before being defeated at the Battle of Chalons. This fierce "sacker of cities," as he was known, also drove the western emperor Valentinian III from his capital at Ravenna in 452.

To this day, Attila is remembered for his cruelty and his warrior spirit. The Huns and the later Mongols may have been the model for *Star Trek*'s Klingons—the warrior tribe that seeks death in battle as a way to win honor. Though his mighty empire died with him, Attila the Hun remains a legendary figure in human history, a man who pushed hard and took what he wanted. He was a one percenter.

THE MONGOLS

It is almost impossible to hear the word Mongol without automatically attaching the word "horde" to it. Most of us imagine the thirteenth century Mongols as barbarous murderers out to pillage, rape, and destroy. This perception is no doubt based on Persian, Chinese, and Russian accounts of the speed and ruthlessness with which the Mongols of old sacked and pillaged their way to become one of the largest empires in world history.

This nomadic people basically produced everything they needed from their livestock herds. The term "Mongol" can be considered a generic reference to warriors fighting in the Middle East, China, and Eastern and Central Europe during that period, because it was applied to soldiers and generals who fought under the identity of Mongols, regardless of whether or not they originated in Mongolia.

Just as a Mongol became "one" with his war pony, modern bikers are "one" with their machines.

Just as the Huns had their Attila, the Mongols have become synonymous with the name of one man: Genghis Khan. When Khan was born in the late twelfth century, Mongolia was divided into many small tribes and tribal chiefs were constantly fighting each other for power. Small-scale wars erupted all the time. In fact, young Genghis could not remember a time when he was not fighting for his life and for that of his people.

His life was the stuff of legend, a life writ large. Khan's wife was kidnapped by enemies of his father known as the Merkits and he had to rescue her (sounds like the start of a great movie). The kidnapping was carried out as revenge on Khan's father for marrying Khan's mother. It seems that Khan's father, Yesugei, had interrupted an arranged marriage with a Merkit groom and made off with the bride-to-be to make her his own. This act started a feud that lasted for generations.

Once Genghis Khan gained power, he formed a union of tribes and forbade inter-tribe raids. These tribes adopted the name of the "never defeated" tribe: the Mongols. Times were harder than any of us could possibly imagine, and the Mongols relied on trade to stay alive. If their traders were preyed upon by other peoples, Khan's Mongols would descend on them and their retribution would be swift and brutal. Besides the Mongol's livestock, raids and war provided the items to trade for goods to improve harsh living conditions. With the establishment of the Mongol empire, trade was secure and boomed throughout Eurasia.

Supposedly, Genghis Khan never initiated war or attacked any country without good reason. Before a war, Khan would send word to the country's king asking for surrender. If the king agreed to Khan's terms there would be no human loss. However, if somebody messed with his messengers or traders, it was likely the last thing they would ever do against him. Sounds like an outlaw club to me.

When raiding other tribes, the aim was to gain strength. The conquered tribe would have to pay tribute and give over its troops to the Mongols. All valuables of the plundered city would be added to the Mongols' stores and only useful people, such as craftsmen, were allowed to live. Upper class city dwellers were usually put to the sword. Khan would always allow a few survivors to escape and spread the word that the Mongols were bad asses. Word of their savagery preceded them and often bloodshed was not necessary, as the Mongols would meet no resistance. In such a case, Khan usually left the town unharmed; he simply demanding

In all places and times, rebellious tribes marked their line in the sand and bellowed, "None but men of valor shall pass."

that they pay him tribute in goods. This led to Khan collecting taxes in an ongoing fashion. Today, we call that protection money.

If the Mongol way of life laid a foundation that would carry through to modern outlaw bikers, their specially bred little horses were the choppers of the time. Mongol horses were small and accustomed to the cold and harsh temperatures in which they fought. Their riders wore light leather armor and were able to move with great speed and agility. The Mongols also invented the stirrup, which allowed them to move and maneuver their horses quickly. How many times since the iron horse emerged have outlaw bikers roared into and out of trouble on bikes customized for speed? Khan's men grew up with horses and hunting, making them better warriors than those raised in agricultural societies. The Mongols' main weapon was the bow and arrow and their skill as archers combined with brilliant horsemanship made them devastating foes.

The Mongols continued their disciplined and superbly coordinated invasions through Western Asia and toward Europe until Khan's death in 1227. The great raider passed the torch of leadership to his third son, Ogedei, who continued the Mongol expansion into Northeastern Asia, conquering Northern China.

The armies of the Mongols reached Poland, Hungary, and Egypt by 1241, when Ogedei Khan died suddenly. Nearly a decade later, Mongka Khan, grandson of Genghis and nephew of Ogedei, took the throne but, by this time, the Western expansion had lost its momentum.

The Khan bloodline and the Mongol nation continued to wreak havoc, however. In 1253 a huge army led by Hulagu Khan attacked the Muslim capitals of Baghdad and Cairo. Baghdad was conquered in 1258, with the city's Christians being spared and the Abbasid caliph killed. However, while the troops were on the road to Cairo in 1259, Mongka Khan died and much of the army returned home to pick a new leader. Mamluk troops repelled the renewed Mongol attack in 1260, in the Battle of Ain Jalut. This marked the farthest west the Mongol Empire would progress.

Kublai Khan succeeded Mongka Khan and moved the Mongol court to Beijing, favoring warmer weather. There, he formed the Yuan dynasty and re-started the invasion of China, in the first war fought with guns on both sides. After 18 years, Kublai Khan conquered both Northern and Southern China, forming the largest land empire in history. Not bad for what began as a small tribe of rebellious one percenters.

THE VIKINGS

Never before has such a terror appeared in Britain as we have now suffered from a pagan race, nor was it thought possible that such an inroad from the sea could be made.

— ALCUIN, ENGLISH SCHOLAR, IN 793 A.D. WHEN HE
HEARD OF THE VIKING RAID ON LINDISFARNE

Few groups spur the fearful imagination of the general public more than a tribe of screaming, axe-wielding Vikings. In fact, the modern image of the outlaw biker shares many similarities with this famous group of hell raisers. Yes, the Vikings were seafaring warriors and robbers (making them pirates), but they were also farmers, traders, and craftspeople from countries that are today known as Sweden, Norway, Denmark, and Iceland. Their wild appearance and love of freedom are hallmarks of the outlaw biker.

The Danish Vikings made the ass-kicking charts in the 800s when they conquered England, Ireland, and Scotland. At about the same time, the Swedish Vikings traveled east to Russia and the Norwegian Vikings sailed to the Americas. Unlike the Huns and the Mongols, the Vikings were not a tribe that expanded through warfare under the command of a charismatic leader such as Attila or Genghis. Rather the Nordic people ventured out to explore the world and discover—and conquer—new lands.

Viking ships set out hundreds of years before their Spanish counterparts, journeying to Italy, Spain, Morocco, and the Holy Land. From the Baltic they penetrated the Continent, traveling up Russian rivers and waterways to the Black Sea and the Caspian Sea, and all the way to Baghdad. In Asia, they met caravans from China and traded walrus ivory and furs for spices, silver, and exotic goods.

They sailed the whole of the North Atlantic and discovered the Faeroes, Iceland, and Greenland, and settled parts of England, Scotland, Ireland, and Normandy—an area that still bears their name (the Danish and Norwegian Vikings who settled this part of France were called Normans, meaning the people from the north). A Scandinavian settlement has even been discovered in Newfoundland, Canada.

Why did the Vikings set forth in such great numbers? Some have cited overpopulation in their native lands; others have looked to the Icelandic sagas, which suggest that tyranny among the powers controlling the Viking

Peter Fonda once said that the only two things that are distinctly American are rock 'n' roll and Harley-Davidson. Add to that the one percenter.

territories sparked mass emigration across the sea. It is also possible that limited available land for farming caused a certain amount of Viking expansion. Perhaps the real lure was the quest for freedom. One thing is certain: Viking shipbuilding technology and advanced navigational skills allowed these people to travel farther and faster than any other race before them had dared.

In battle, the Vikings were fearless, especially the elite fighters known as Berserkers. If the Vikings were one percenters, these warriors who believed that death in battle was a sure way to Valhalla, which offered a heavenly afterlife of wine, women, and song, were the Vikings' filthy few. It was the Berserkers who gave the Vikings their reputation for savagery. They were believed to have possessed the souls of animals, and their only purpose in battle was to kill anything and everything that crossed their paths. Twentieth century neurologist Howard Douglas Fabing described Berserkergang—the state of mind in which Berserkers fought—as:

> This fury, which was called berserkergang, occurred not only in the heat of battle, but also during laborious work. Men who were thus seized performed things which otherwise seemed impossible for human power. This condition is said to have begun with shivering, chattering of the teeth, and chill in the body, and then the face swelled and changed its color. With this was connected a great hot-headedness, which at last gave over into a great rage, under which they howled as wild animals, bit the edge of their shields, and cut down everything they met without discriminating between friend or foe. When this condition ceased, a great dulling of the mind and feebleness followed, which could last for one or several days.

Anyone who has ever been to a really good one percenter party can tell you a thing or two about berserkergang.

The Norsemen were known for their cruelty in battle, devising bizarre and twisted tortures for their surviving enemies. One such famous torture was known as "red wings," or "blood wings." Today's outlaw bikers also have a ritual that goes by the same name, but it is an entirely different thing. (We'll go into that later.) The Scandinavian raiders who employed the red wings form of torture would stretch an enemy around a tree and secure his limbs, then cut open his back and pull his lungs out through the cuts. The bloody lungs would billow with each of the man's last breaths, making his lungs look like flapping red wings. Talk about your mean muthas.

With their wild visage, monstrous battle axes, inventive ways of striking fear, such as making their ships look like dragons, the Vikings certainly knew how to instill terror in the hearts and minds of their opponents. It is easy to see why, hundreds of years later, they continue to fascinate the bad boy in all of us. They were one percenters.

MERCENARY KNIGHTS

Where there is war, in all times and places, there is work to be done for those whose business is death. So, there have always been mercenaries. During the medieval period of the fourteenth century, the area now known as Germany was a mix of feuding cities, kingdoms, and republics. These all theoretically fell under the authority of the King of Germany. He in turn was under the authority of the Holy Roman Emperor. The reality was that the King of Germany could be, and on occasion was, deposed by the princes of Germany and replaced by their choice. The same was also true for the Holy Roman Emperor, who was open to disposition and replacement by the Electors. It was a time of constant feuds and wars—a perfect breeding place for mercenaries.

Towns and cities of a particular area often banded together for protection. These threats could be from local robber knights, but as often as not the threats came from their own overlords. The instability of the region meant towns tended to have some form of fortifications and a town militia for defense. The town militia was raised and drilled by neighborhoods of the town. Each neighborhood was expected to provide, arm, and train a certain number of troops to fight for their immediate neighborhood.

By the fifteenth century many of the larger cities had their own artillery. These were often commanded and crewed by mercenaries since they usually had the required skills. The use of mercenaries to supplement and, in some cases, replace the militia became an increasingly common practice. The obvious disadvantage was the possibility of treachery or desertions should they not pay the mercenaries.

In many places a League of Knights was created, offering its services to the highest bidders. Many of these leagues were little more than robber

Rip Rose was the roving reporter for Easyriders *magazine. He was a true one percenter and knight of the road.*

bands and they preyed heavily on the local populations, causing more destruction than they prevented.

Republics were areas situated in inhospitable parts of Germany. The most famous of the republics was the Eternal Alliance of Swiss Cantons. From 1308 the Eternal Alliance was a permanent and important ally of the Holy Roman Empire. Austria and Burgundy attempted to reclaim lost lands from the Swiss Cantons and both failed. However, for the rest of the Holy Roman Empire the Swiss republic was a vital source of mercenaries; even the emperor employed Swiss mercenary troops.

The other Republics relied upon local able-bodied men for their defense. As a result, most armies were composed of farmers, armed only with spears or weapons improvised from agricultural equipment and with little or no armor. Well folks, guess who usually won.

The anarchy that ranged over much of the Holy Roman Empire made it a fertile recruiting ground for mercenaries and a ready source of employment. All types of mercenary units plied their trade in the empire. From the thirteenth century, German mercenary knights were for hire around Europe and had a formidable reputation.

The most desired mercenary fighters were the crossbowmen and archers, trained to fight in a close group, using volley fire to break up and disrupt enemy units. The increasing use of artillery also saw master gunners offering their services for hire. Cities frequently hired such gunners to oversee their cannons. Some were offered a year's salary as a bonus if they successfully repelled an assault.

It was the heavy foot soldier, however, who was the most sought after mercenary. Up until the mid-fifteenth century, these were armored spearmen who were usually capable of withstanding the charge of knights. The adoption of pikes by the Swiss Cantons altered the form of mercenary knights throughout Europe. Using mass infantry formations armed with pikes, the Swiss were able to inflict a series of stinging defeats on their opponents. The effectiveness of the Swiss led to them becoming highly desired as mercenaries. These were hard men, killing was their business, and prey meant pay. In other words, the flamboyant guards surrounding the Pope in their funky hats and pantaloons are one percenters, or at least they were back in the day.

PIRATES

*In an honest service, there are commonly low wages and hard
labour; in this [piracy] plenty, satiety, pleasure and ease, liberty, and
power; and who would not balance creditor on this side, when all the
hazard that is run for it at worst, is only a sour look or two at choking
[hanging]? No, a merry life and a short one shall be my motto.*

—Attributed to Captain Bartholomew
"Black Bart" Roberts (1720)

A pirate is someone who robs and plunders by sea and, as you might imagine, there have been pirates for as long as there have been boats and ships. Accounts of piratical raiding stretch back to 150 B.C. when Cicilia in the Mediterranean flourished as a pirate haven. Because of piratical poetry, plays, stories, and movies, the romantic image of the swashbuckling sea rover or buccaneer is generally centered around the golden age of piracy—around 1630 to 1730 A.D., the time of the pirates of the Caribbean.

Many outlaw bikers feel an affinity with pirates, for these seamen of old lived by a code of ethics very similar to that of the one percenter. In a time in which serving with the Royal Navy was much like being on a floating prison, "going on account" as a pirate meant freedom at sea. In fact, a pirate ship offered one of the first real democracies for its multiracial crew. Aboard ship, every scallywag had an equal say as to where they would sail in search of prizes and every man got an equal share of the booty.

Pirates lived hard and died young, and like outlaw bikers, they lived for today, partying their spoils away as soon as they got them. Like Black Bart said, "a short but merry life." The image of the murdering pirate who spent all his pieces of eight on rum in the taverns of Tortuga and Port Royal and his nights with loose strumpets is an accurate one.

Many of the more well-known pirates from the golden age of piracy only plied their trade as a rover for a few short years before being put to death for their crimes. Even the infamous Blackbeard (Edward Teach) only went a-pirating for 15 months before swinging by the neck from the bowsprit of Lieutenant Robert Maynard's ship, the *Pearl*, in 1718. Likewise, Captain John "Calico" Rackham's Caribbean exploits as a pirate only lasted from 1718 to 1720 before his ship was taken along with his crew and the famous lady pirates Anne Bonny and Mary Read.

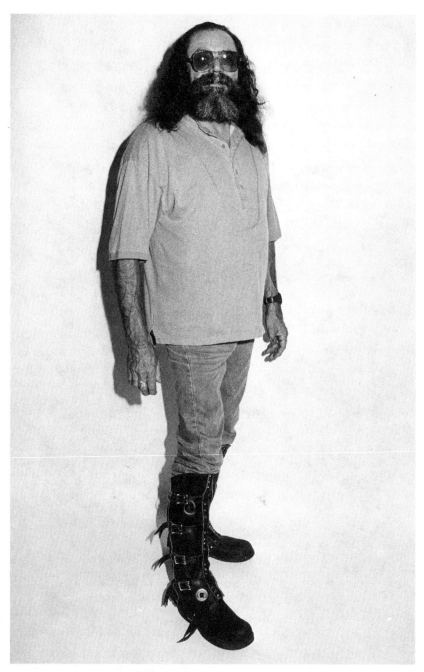

In this shot of Rip at the Easyriders office, it's easy to see the resemblance between scooter tramps and badass buccaneers.

Skulls and crossbones are as much a part of biker lore as that of the foreboding "colors" flown by pirates.

But the image of the free-spirited buccaneer stirs the heart of every out-law biker, for their common love is freedom and both share a distaste for the straight and narrow path. As Peter Fonda said in his role as Heavenly Blues in the Roger Corman film *Wild Angels*, "We just want to be free to ride our machines without being hassled by the man."

Today we live in a restrictive Big Brother society in which the nanny state rules over our every move. We cannot drive a car without wearing a seatbelt; we cannot ride a motorcycle without wearing a helmet; we cannot cross the street anywhere except in the areas clearly marked for crossing. I heard of a recent law restricting children from playing "tag" at schools because there was a chance that a kid might fall down and the parents would sue the school. It seems we exist in a time of insane litigation, ridiculous regulations, and safety Nazis who monitor us for our own good. It is a time when our liberties are freely given away under the guise of something called Homeland Security. What we have instead is the illusion of freedom and security, both produced by the media in much the same way that Dustin Hoffman produces the media manipulations of a fake war in the film, *Wag the Dog*.

Naturally, when freedom is restricted, the rebel in all of us steps for-ward. It is no wonder that the highest opening box office gross of all time as of 2006 went to *Pirates of the Caribbean II: Dead Man's Chest*. You see, there's a bit of Johnny Depp's Captain Jack Sparrow in all of us. We all have a bit of larceny within us itching to get out. For the one percenter, free rein is given to hear the beating of that black heart within. We are also searching for those illusive freedoms that we fear are dwindling.

We are in fact a nation of pirates. After all, many sailed to America to escape one form of restricted rule or another in favor of freedom. Once we got here, we soon set out to steal the land from the natives, taking whatever they had that was worth stealing. It is no coincidence that we use the terms "hostile takeover" and "corporate raiders" in modern business dealings. The essence of business in many ways is piracy, or as Captain Jack Sparrow's pirate toast proclaims, "Take what you can, give nothing back."

It is easy to see why bikers may be likened to pirates. Not only do we find many bikers sporting piratical tattoos, but many pirate traditions are shared by the modern one percenter. Take the appearance of a biker with his long, free flowing hair, bandanna, and beard. The freedom of the sea is much like the freedom of the road, where adventure is found at every turn and the great expanse of America stretches out before you like the endless sea.

Members of outlaw bike clubs wear a patch on the back of their leathers or on cut-off denim that is proudly proclaimed as their club "colors." The origin of these colors were the flags flown by pirate and privateering ships marking the personal flag of the ship's captain. For hundreds of years, these colors were red flags, which were struck to let opponents know that "no quarter would be given or taken," meaning that the prey should expect no mercy but out-and-out bloodshed in the taking of their ship. Red banners gave us the term Jolly Roger from the French *le jolie rouge*, or "pretty red." By 1700 this evolved into the white skull and crossbones being used on a black flag as the banner for piracy. Every pirate captain had his own set of colors, as unique as those worn by one percenter clubs. These various black flags held many of the images still used by outlaws today—the skull with crossed bones or cutlasses, skeletons, devils, an hourglass symbolizing that your time is up, and so on. To "strike your colors," then and now, was a way to show the world your standard and banner. In both cases the message is clear: Mess with us at your own peril.

By the mid-eighteenth century the golden age of pirates in the Atlantic had come to an end. The borders of the once endless map had been drawn in and charted. Where there were once great unknown expanses of sea marked on maps as "beyond here, there be dragons," the edges of the world became known and the hiding places of pirates were revealed. The royalty of Europe and the governors of America sent warships to root out the last of the Caribbean pirates. With Blackbeard's bloody death in 1718 and the hanging of John Rackham in 1720, the wild days of freebooting appeared to be over. However, piracy continued in many parts of the world and is still a big problem today in many third world countries. Only nowadays, the pirates have speedboats and rocket launchers.

In fact, there was a great deal of pirating going on during and after the War of Independence. Before this, the Spanish and the French were popular targets for plunder and smuggling, but with the war that earned the American colonies their freedom from Great Britain, English ships became the prizes of plunder. The Continental Congress sanctioned privateers by the hundreds, and nearly any form of ship that would float turned a profit by going "on the account."

For nearly as long as there have been pirates, there have been privateers— men who would sail under Letters of Marque allowing them to ply their trade legally in the office of taking ships of enemy nations. Often, a privateer would be told to split his take of plunder with the country under whose flag and letters he was operating. So, privateering was basically legalized pirating, but the line between the two was dangerously thin, with many a privateer turning pirate when a ship of *any* nation appeared to be a fat prize.

Privateering soon became one of the biggest businesses on the New England coast. Even our own George Washington owned silver cups and china plates that had been taken from British ships by legalized pirates. New York alone fitted out over 100 ships for privateering duty, and these took over 270 British ships by 1820. Pirating became big business, and those who outfitted the privateers tended to keep their share of loot, investing their spoils instead of just frittering them away, as did most pirates, who usually died penniless. Still, in all times and places, the great lures to piracy were that the sea offered adventure and freedom, fortune and glory.

A BRIEF HISTORY OF PIRACY
150 B.C. TO 1820 A.D.

150 B.C.
Cicilia becomes a pirate haven in the Mediterranean.

67 A.D.
Pompey fights off Cicilian pirates.

1200
Letters of Marque allow pirates to become privateers (legalized pirates in service to a particular country).

1492
Columbus lands on the shores of the New World, a fertile shore to pillage.

1494
Treaty of Tordesillas divides the New World between Spain and Portugal—let the raiding begin!

Grabbing the essentials before a run or voyage always includes plenty of beer ... and rum!

1518
Captain Aruj Barbarossa, creator of the Barbary States, is killed by the Spaniards.

1519
Cortes lands in Mexico and proceeds to spread disease and death to the local inhabitants before robbing them blind.

1525–1825
Algiers becomes a haven for Barbary pirates for over 300 years.

1531
Pizarro slaughters the Incas and steals their gold and silver.

1562
John Hawkins makes his first voyage to the Spanish Main.

1572
Captain Francis Drake sacks Nombre de Dios.

1603
Infamous Irish lady pirate Granuaile dies in Rockfleet Castle.

1606
John Ward takes over 100,000 pounds worth of cargo from the ship *Reniera e Soderina*.

1616
Pirate Simon Danzer is executed in Tunis.

1630
Buccaneers take over Tortuga and make it a pirate port.

1668
Captain Henry Morgan sacks Portobello.

1671

Captain Morgan raids Panama.

1688

Morgan dies peacefully . . . drunk.

1690

Madagascar becomes a famous pirate port for over 30 years.

1695

Captain Henry Avery takes the Moghul of India's ship *Ganj-i-Sawai*, plundering over 300,000 pounds in treasure.

1701

Pirate-hunter–turned-pirate Captain William Kidd is hanged with his crew at Execution Dock in London.

1704

Captain John Quelch (one of the first to fly the black flag that became known as the Jolly Roger) is executed.

1718

Edward "Blackbeard" Teach is hanged following a fierce hand-to-hand battle with Lieutenant Maynard of the Royal Navy.

1718

Captain Edward England takes ships and plunders the waters of the Atlantic and Indian oceans.

1719

Captain John Roberts, also known as Bartholomew Roberts, takes prizes in Atlantic and Caribbean waters.

1719

Captain Howell Davis is ambushed and killed near Principe Island.

Where would a biker be without his leathers? They act as a second skin should the rider go over the high side.

1720
Captain John "Calico Jack" Rackham is hanged with his crew.

1721
Female pirate Mary Read dies of fever in prison.

1721
Captain Edward Low takes ships for three years in the Atlantic and Caribbean.

1750–1830
Pirates are active in the Persian Gulf, Red Sea, and Indian Ocean for over 80 years.

1807
Famous Chinese pirate leader Ching Yih dies and is succeeded by his infamous wife, Cheng I Sao.

1803–1814
Captain Jean Lafitte raids and plunders ships in the Gulf of Mexico and the Caribbean for nearly 10 years before being pardoned for fighting for Louisiana and the United States.

It is easy to see the wild and free persona of the pirate, the Viking, the Mongol, the Hun, and the mercenary expressed in the rebellious spirit of the outlaw biker as he roars down a stretch of western road, his brothers riding in a tight formation at his side, flying their frightening colors. All are whooping and hollering like Berserkers, celebrating their pure, unadulterated freedom in the wind. Though the image of the one percenter inspires terror in the straight world, the outlaw bikers' scorecard for death and destruction pales mightily when compared to the bloodshed wreaked by their ancient counterparts and distant rebel relatives.

As we have seen, the seeds of rebellion were warmed by the light of freedom and were fed a restrictive diet of conformity until they burst forth on a new land. That fertile land became known as America. On that new shore outcasts and rebels gave birth to their own brand of outlaws.

CHAPTER 2

Amerian Rebels

HOW A COUNTRY FORGED BY REBELS AND OUTCASTS
BRED THEIR OWN BRAND OF OUTLAWS:
THE FRONTIERSMEN AND PIONEERS, THE COWBOYS
AND GUNSLINGERS, THE MOUNTAIN MEN AND BIKERS.

In the early west where life had no value, death sometimes had its price. That is why the bounty hunters appeared.
—FROM THE INTRODUCTION OF *FOR A FEW DOLLARS MORE*

The image of the outlaw biker is a distinctly American phenomenon. The origin of the rough, leather-clad hellion on two wheels was born in the late 1940s, but we need to peer nearly 200 years into the past to witness the birth of this rebellious breed.

Only a small portion—13 British colonies—of the great expanse of land that would become known as America was occupied by Europeans at this time. It was a time of discovery and wonder, as well as of mayhem and death.

The American Revolution, funded in part by the French, resulted in the creation of a new nation in 1776. The birth of the United States of America marked the triumph of rebels over the status quo in England; new democratic thought overthrew the reign of monarchs. These new democratic ideals soon took hold of the minds and hearts of American society.

As we all remember from grade school, the Revolutionary Era began in 1763, when the British imposed a series of taxes considered illegal by the colonists. After protests in Boston, the British sent over troops to enforce these taxes and met head on with the colonial militia in 1775. The British fought in a traditional, uptight fashion, wearing bright red coats and marching in a straight line. They were easy pickin's for the Patriot Militia, which would hide in the woods and shoot from behind rocks, trees, and everywhere. Yes, the Americans fought dirty, but so did the British.

In 1775, the British Army consisted of about 36,000 men worldwide, but wartime recruitment steadily increased that number. Over the course of the war, the British hired more than 30,000 soldiers as mercenaries; they were called Hessians because many of them came from Hesse-Kassel. Interestingly, there is an infamous motorcycle club with the same name. Germans made up about one-third of the British troop strength in North America. By 1779, the number of British and German troops stationed in North America was over 60,000.

Nearly 20 percent of the colonies' population were British loyalists, which meant that the Patriot Militia had the support of over 80 percent of the population, so the Brits could only hold onto a few coastal cities. Long story short, the 13 colonies became the first 13 states in these United States under the banner of the Declaration of Independence. The French formed an alliance with the United States in 1778 and America used the French Navy and Army to even the odds against the British troops. The combined forces took Saratoga from the British in 1777 and Yorktown in 1781, leading to the Treaty of Paris in 1783. Thus, the United States was finally recognized as an independent nation. It was a nation born of rebellion as well as robbery, piracy, and plunder—the perfect breeding ground for independent spirits of all kinds. It was into this new country that the frontiersman was born.

FRONTIERSMEN AND PIONEERS

The image of one percenter bikers hearkens back to the rough individuals who dared to go where no man had gone before. This was a breed of man who dared to take that empty-handed leap into the void—wild, untamed, free spirits setting out to claim the ill-conceived concept of manifest destiny.

The frontiersman was of this ilk. When thinking of the early United States of America and the settling of the early west, three men come instantly to mind: Daniel Boone, Davy Crockett, and Jim Bowie. Many American myths and legends grew up around these three.

*It's hard to separate the American biker from the frontiersman and cowboy image. Brother
Rogue is proof of that.*

Born in 1734 in Berks County, Pennsylvania, Daniel Boone embodied the soul of the pioneer and explorer. Known for clearing the Wilderness Road in 1775, Boone established the settlements of Boonesborough and Boone's Station in Kentucky.

Many Native Americans sided with the British during the Revolutionary War, and Boone fought proudly against the British and the Shawnee tribe. There have been many stories about how Daniel Boone used the Indian's warrior tactics against them. In modern times he is depicted as a wild man himself, wearing deerskin clothes and carrying a war hatchet.

As a boy he came to know the friendly Indians in the forest and learned to hunt from them using a crude spear. When he was 12 his father gave him a rifle and his career as a huntsman began.

Davy Crockett shares a public image similar to Daniel Boone's. (Crockett may have even worn a coonskin cap, though Boone most certainly did not; Boone thought the hats, which were popular among hunters of the era, ridiculous.) Born in 1786 near Limestone, Kentucky, Crockett is best known for his bear hunting skills and incredible marksmanship with a rifle. His valor included fighting under Andrew Jackson in the Creek Indian War and boldly fighting and dying while defending the Alamo in 1836 at the age of 49.

What is perhaps less known is that Crockett had a keen sense of humor. His wit and wisdom led to his serving in the state legislature and the Congress for the state of Tennessee. His motto was, "Be always sure you are right, then go ahead."

Jim Bowie, inventor of the Bowie knife, was born in 1795 in Georgia. He was another wild man known for being bold and brazen. Bowie lived in Louisiana for many years and owned much land. He moved to Texas in 1823 and married the governor's daughter. He also died at the Alamo in 1836 while commanding the defense against Santa Anna's forces.

Before the revolution in Texas, Bowie took part in many adventures. He spent considerable time cultivating friendships with Indians in his search for the elusive silver and gold reported to be hidden in the interior of Texas. By some accounts, he is said to have found the fabled San Saba mines, also known as the Bowie mines, near the geographic center of present day Texas.

By their words, deeds, and amazing exploits, these three early Americans were one percenters in a new land of infinite possibility.

COWBOYS AND GUNSLINGERS

The story of the American Wild West is very much the story of those seeking the edges of known reality in hopes of finding freedom and fortune beyond the bounds of convention. America's history is rich with a diverse cast of interesting characters, all of whom inspired the modern image of the outlaw biker.

Rugged mountain men, such as Christopher "Kit" Carson and Jim Bridger, and pistol-packin' legends, such as Buffalo Bill Cody and Anne Oakley, stir the imagination with their storied exploits in taming the great American West. True Wild West bad boys and outlaws, such as Jesse James and Billy the Kid, lit the fires of rebellion in the heart of the tribe that would become known as bikers.

Ask any biker to name 10 favorite actors and you can bet Clint Eastwood and John Wayne will be on that list—both known for their work in numerous western films. The true-life legends that inspired the fiction of penny dreadfuls, dime-store novels, and western shoot 'em up movies all breathe life into the biker image and deserve their share of homage in this book. Let's look at a few American Western legends as well as bad boys who have acted as inspirations for the one percenter.

Kit Carson became a living legend in the early nineteenth century as a trapper, scout, mountain man, and soldier. Carson spent his childhood in Boone's Lick, Missouri. His father died when he was nine years old, which led to his apprenticeship with a saddle maker and prevented him from going to school. At age 14 Kit left Missouri for Sante Fe, New Mexico, and became a famous fur-trapper, leading expeditions near Taos from 1823 to 1831. In the early 1840s he was employed as a hunter at Bent's Fort. But as often happened with white trappers, Kit immersed himself in the world of the Native Americans, even marrying an Arapahoe and, later, a member of the Cheyenne tribe.

Kit Carson earned his fame (and infamy) through his courage in the expansion of the West. In 1842 he became a guide for John C. Fremont and helped trail-blaze the way to Oregon and California. Then Fremont joined California's Bear Flag Rebellion before the outbreak of the Mexican-American War in 1846, the war in which Carson led American forces and became a national hero.

After the war, Kit returned to New Mexico to drive sheep to California, where gold rush prices paid him a pretty penny. He was appointed federal

Loaded for bear, this scooter tramp has a warm spot for the Old West.

Indian agent for Northern New Mexico in 1853 and retained this post until the Civil War called him to action in 1861. Carson helped organize the New Mexico volunteer infantry and led a brutal war against the Navajo people.

Sadly, he is also remembered for leading over 8,000 Navajo men, women, and children on what has become known as the Long Walk—a 300-mile trek across Arizona to Fort Sumner in New Mexico. The U.S. government sent Colonel Kit Carson to gather the Navajo together and move them to Fort Sumner. When the Indians refused to move, Carson destroyed their crops and livestock, burnt their villages, and killed many of them. The people of the Navajo Nation finally relented, and in 1864 Carson led between 8,000 and 9,000 Native Americans to Fort Sumner. Along the 300-mile trip to the camp, about 200 people died of cold and starvation. Many more people died after they arrived at the barren reservation, which was unsuitable for raising crops.

William Frederick Cody was born in Iowa in 1846. The trapper, pony express rider, stagecoach driver, and Civil War soldier earned the nickname Buffalo Bill at the age of 22 for his skill at slaughtering buffaloes. He sold the meat to the Kansas Pacific Railroad to feed its workers.

The U.S. Army used Bill as a scout from 1868 to 1872 and he was awarded the Congressional Medal of Honor for hazardous duty in the Indian Wars. In 1872 Buffalo Bill became a showman, reenacting his encounters with the Indians on the stage in a show called "Scouts of the Prairie." He started his Wild West show in 1883 with real cowboys and Indians shooting and hollering their way to stardom before live crowds. The show was a big hit in Europe, spending a third of its 30-year run entertaining people who could not conceive of the exploits that took place in the savage Wild West. By the turn of the century, Buffalo Bill was one of the most famous and recognizable men on the planet.

The Wild West Show was popular largely because the Wild West itself was slipping into extinction. People felt a nostalgia for the fading American frontier. As America became civilized and the last gunslingers were erased from the vast prairies, Buffalo Bill's Wild West show offered a glimpse into an outlaw world that was no more.

Though he helped the government to drive Native Americans from their land, Buffalo Bill eventually used his fame to focus on Indian rights. He once said, "Every Indian outbreak that I have ever known has resulted from broken promises and broken treaties by the government."

Billy the Kid, also known as Patrick Henry McCarty and William Henry Bonney, hailed from a very unlikely place for a man who would go on to epitomize the Wild West outlaw; he was born in New York City in 1859. Billy's father died around the end of the Civil War and his mother, Catherine, contracted tuberculosis. In 1873 she married William Antrim and moved the family to Silver City, New Mexico, hoping the drier climate would help her cope with her disease. But her condition continued to worsen until she died in 1874.

Billy and his brother, Joseph, were placed in separate foster homes and Billy found work waiting tables at a local hotel. He was arrested for hiding a bundle of laundry as a prank on a Chinese laundryman. After two days in jail, Billy wormed his way up a jailhouse chimney and escaped. He was a fugitive from the law . . . and lived the rest of his life as an outlaw.

The notorious Hole in the Wall Gang or just a few brothers out for a weekend putt?

In 1877 Billy found work as a civilian teamster at Camp Grant Army Post, hauling lumber to a mill. The blacksmith at the camp, one Frank Cahil, loved to pick on Billy. Bad idea. After Cahil berated the Kid and threw him to the ground, Billy shot and killed him. Billy once again escaped imprisonment at the camp's guardhouse and was on the run.

Apache Indians stole Billy's horse, forcing him to walk many miles through the wilderness. He turned up at the home of Heiskell Jones in Pecos Valley, near death. Mrs. Jones nursed the outlaw back to health and the Jones family developed a strong attachment to Billy, giving him one of their horses. As an outlaw unable to find honest work, Billy met up with another outlaw named Jesse Evans, leader of a gang of cattle rustlers known as the Boys, and joined them.

As is often the case in a good western tale, revenge soon entered the picture. After fighting in the Lincoln County War, Billy worked for a time with

One percenters face discrimination and threats to their liberty with every mile they ride and every twist of the road.

a man named John Tunstall. Tunstall treated Billy well and was a true friend. When he was gunned down by a deputy sheriff in 1878, Billy swore to avenge his friend, tracking down and killing the deputy as well as the county sheriff, William Brady.

Now more wanted than ever, Billy took to stealing livestock from ranchers and Apaches. In 1879, territorial governor and retired Union general, Lee Wallace, offered all those who took part in the Lincoln County War amnesty. Billy met with Wallace and agreed to testify in a court of law against certain combatants. Part of the agreement included a short stay in jail for Billy. But after Billy testified, the district attorney refused to set him free. The Kid managed to slip out of his handcuffs and fled.

For nearly a year, Billy hung out around Fort Sumner and became friends with a bartender named Pat Garrett. Later, Garrett was elected sheriff of Lincoln County and was charged with arresting his friend Billy. By this time Billy had formed his own gang, known as the Rustlers.

By the end of 1880, Governor Wallace put a $500 reward out for Billy, and Pat Garrett began his famous pursuit of the outlaw. As the story goes, Pat Garrett set many traps for Billy and his gang, but the outlaw seemed to always be a step ahead. Billy's luck finally ran out on December 23, 1880, when Garrett and his deputies tracked the outlaws to their hideout in Stinking Springs (lovely name), surrounded them, and lay siege for two days before Billy and his gang waved the white flag.

Billy was jailed near Santa Fe, New Mexico, and sentenced to death for his many crimes. However, Billy still had one miraculous escape left in him, killing two guards in the process. Then, on July 14, 1881, Pat Garrett was questioning Billy's friend, Peter Maxwell, in Maxwell's darkened bedroom. Billy unexpectedly walked in but couldn't see Garrett in the dim light. Pat pulled his revolver and shot Billy twice, once in the heart. Billy the Kid died having been credited for the killing of 21 men, one for every year of his short life.

Few folk heroes have been loved as real-life Robin Hoods during their lifetime; Jesse Woodson James, born on September 5, 1847, was one of them. At the end of the Wild West era, Jesse is remembered for rebelling against society and robbing from the rich.

Jesse's parents lived in Clay County, Missouri, with his older brother Frank and younger sister Susan. His father was a Baptist minister who served as a chaplain on a wagon train bound for California during the gold rush. Reverend James died from drinking contaminated water during the trip in 1850 and the family returned to their farm in Missouri. Jesse's mother Zerelda eventually married a well-to-do doctor, Archie Reuben Samuel, from whom Frank and Jesse learned horseback riding and shooting. While Frank was more "bookish" by nature growing up, Jesse was ever the charming prankster.

During the Civil War, residents of Missouri were allowed to serve the armies on either side because while many settlers came from the South and owned slaves (including the James family), Missouri's economy was linked to the North. In 1861, Frank James enlisted in the Confederate Army. After the Battle of Lexington, Frank joined Quantrill's Raiders, known for their guerilla tactics, and was with Quantrill at the bloody sacking of Lawrence, Kansas.

Three months after the raid on Lawrence, Union soldiers questioned a 15-year-old Jesse James and horse-whipped him for refusing to answer questions. This incident led Jesse to join the guerilla forces of Quantrill lieutenant "Bloody" Bill Anderson, and Jesse and Frank were part of the raid on Centralia, Missouri, in 1864. Like a scene out of a 1970s biker movie, over 100 armed raiders rode into town to rob the train. While waiting, they terrorized the citizens, robbing and burning stores, and robbing the passengers waiting at the station. When the train arrived they pulled 24 wounded Union soldiers from the train and murdered them in front of the community. They then set the train on fire and sent it west with no crew aboard to crash and burn. Federal troops followed the raiders but Bloody Bill and his men bushwhacked the infantry, killing over 120 troops. Jesse himself was said to have killed eight men that day.

After the Civil War, Jesse settled down with his aunt in Kansas City and fell in love with his first cousin, Zee (named Zerelda after Jesse's mother). He was known as a dapper dresser and attended church often. But Frank and Jesse soon turned to crime, saying that they were forced to be outlaws because their family was persecuted for owning slaves. The James brothers led a gang of outlaws, which included the Younger brothers and other ex-confederates. Jesse felt justified in his outlaw pursuits, stealing from the industrial North like a Wild West Robin Hood. His gang robbed their way across the West for over 15 years.

The James-Younger Gang successfully robbed nine banks before turning to robbing stagecoaches and trains. In 1866, a man named John Newman began writing dime-store novels that glorified the violent deeds of

Jesse and the gang. Even though the gang often killed innocent bystanders at their crime scenes, they were the rock stars of their generation and adored by many civilized city dwellers in the East. The same romanticized appeal for the bad man would later spawn outlaw biker books and exploitation films like Roger Corman's *The Wild Angels*.

American journalists during the late nineteenth century exaggerated the James Gang's crimes, turning Jesse's harassment of railroad executives known for taking private lands for their railroads into the romantic notion that Jesse was some sort of Robin Hood. In a time when gunslingers were becoming extinct, Jesse and his gang's exploits gave the mystique of the Wild West one last hurrah. Tales of the gang's deeds were only made more dashing by the many times it pulled the wool over the eyes of the Pinkerton Detective Agency, whose agents pursued Jesse and Frank for many years.

After nine years of courtship, Jesse married Zee in 1874 and the couple honeymooned in Galveston, Texas. Frank married Annie Ralston in Omaha, and the two brothers settled down for a while, though they were blamed for nearly every robbery of any size that occurred in the West at that time.

The Pinkertons continued to search for Jesse, even using an undercover agent named Jack Ladd as a farmhand, who lived next door to the James family farm. In January 1875, Ladd thought he saw Frank and Jesse at the farm house and tossed a smoke bomb into the main room. A young boy named Archie Samuel thought the bomb was a loose stick from the fire and threw it back into the fireplace and the bomb exploded, killing the boy. The blast also wounded Jesse's mother and her hand was later amputated. Newspapers reported the incident and the public were enraged at the Pinkerton's tactics.

A few months later, Jesse, Frank, and the Younger brothers tried to rob a northern bank in Northfield, Minnesota. Jesse shot a bank cashier and the noise raised the bank alarm. Citizens of Northfield opened fire on the gang and the Younger brothers were badly wounded, while the James boys managed to escape.

After putting together a new gang, the James brothers staged robberies in Kentucky, Alabama, and Missouri. After the gang's last train robbery in 1881, Jesse moved his family to St. Joseph, Missouri, and settled under the name Tom Howard. At that time, Jesse had a $10,000 reward on his head, big money in those days. Jesse planned on retiring right after one last, big bank robbery in Platte County.

Just as an outlaw of the Old West looked lost without his horse, a biker seems out of place without his chopper.

On April 3, 1882, Jesse was in his home, planning the bank robbery with two brothers he had worked with before, Bob and Charles Ford. He noticed that a picture on the wall was crooked and got up on a chair to straighten it. Bob took the opportunity to shoot Jesse just below his right ear. Zee heard the gunshot and ran into the room, trying to stop the blood, but Jesse was dead. He was 34 years old.

It was later discovered that Bob Ford made a deal with Governor Thomas Crittenden to kill Jesse. In return, Ford was to be given amnesty for his many crimes and the $10,000 reward on Jesse's head.

Over a period of 15 years, Jesse and his gang committed 26 holdups and made off with more than $200,000. Legend has it that he killed 17 men. Billy the Kid and Jesse James were one percenters, not because of their violence or skill as death dealers, but because they lived life on their own terms, outside of the law and society's norm.

Any time society breeds a nation of sheep—when people grow too lazy or meek or subservient to power—a few wolves emerge to attack these weaknesses and keep the human herd strong. Such is the case with the tribes we have visited thus far. Whether Huns, Mongols, Vikings, pirates, or gun-slinging outlaws, these human wolves define the boundaries of society by their very lawlessness.

You could say that in America today, we live in a society of easily led sheep. While doctors or lawyers might dress up in leather and pretend to be outlaw bikers on the weekend, they are fatted calves dressing up as wolves. When they meet a real wolf . . . well, that's something altogether different. Those living high within society's fences aren't always so comfortable confronting the rebels at the gate—the one percent who live outside the law, the one percent your mother warned you about.

Society always needs its outlaws and bad boys. Even today, one of the last descendants of the James family has made a fortune off the notoriety of his family's lawless history. Jesse Gregory James was a welder and machinist working for an aftermarket motorcycle parts company called Performance Machine when I first met him in 1992. He has since become a household name fostered by his bad boy image. If it is true that ladies love outlaws, then this magical charisma has worked for James. He founded a custom motorcycle shop called West Coast Choppers in Long Beach, California, and created a clothing line that every teenager and custom bike lover in the nation embraced. He went on to star in three TV documentaries about his life called *Motorcycle Mania I, II,* and *III,* and was the host of a TV series on the Discovery Channel called *Monster Garage.* Here, Jesse had the chance to remake ordinary autos into monster machines. The undercurrent of all these programs was Jesse's anti-establishment personality. He became the anti-host. As TV series executive producer Thom Beers once said, "Every woman wants him and every man wants to be like him."

But Jesse had an underlying agenda to his work on TV and it was a noble one. His goal was to let the youth of America know that it's cool to be a blue collar worker and do something creative with your hands. In a time when kids were being mass produced to toil in white collar jobs, working for software companies, Jesse pointed out that it was cool to think outside the cubicle. He even proved that a welder with attitude could get his piece of the American dream and ride into the sunset with the pretty girl—in this case his bride, the beautiful and talented actress Sandra Bullock.

Before we leave the Old West, we should spend a few minutes talking about the effect of western movies and TV series on the collective consciousness. Some of the earliest motion pictures were westerns, going back to *The Great Train Robbery* in 1903. Americans, and especially American boys, have always had a fascination with the lawless Old West. Early TV series revolved around singing cowboys such as Gene Autry and Roy Rogers. These shoot 'em ups always pitted the white hats against the black hats. Good and bad was easily defined by the color of the hat worn, white for the good guys, black for the bad. Today, bikers are notorious for wearing black— black T-shirts, black leather jackets, and black jeans. There is even a T-shirt that proclaims, "Good Guys Wear Black," to show how much the biker image has changed in recent years.

Westerns deal with the conquest of the great American wilderness. The heroes of westerns generally adhere to codes of honor rather than strictly to the Law. The classic western movie usually follows the story of a lone man on a horse as he struggles to do the right thing in a land known for its independence and freedom from oppression. A new kind of film in the 1960s blurred the lines of good and bad, featuring the anti-hero of the early Italian westerns. In these revisionist spaghetti westerns, there were no white hats.

It is no wonder that all manner of bikers, from weekend warrior to one percenter, love the wildly violent Italian westerns of Sergio Leone. He depicted the Early West as a haven for outlaws and gunslingers looking to make a fistful of dollars as mercenaries in a new land. Leone and many

Neither rain nor sleet nor wind will keep this modern day pony express rider from a beer run.

movie makers who came after him developed and exploited a fantasy world of filthy men who were out for themselves at all costs. Even the heroes of these westerns are basically bad guys; they're just the ones who are a little less bad. So, westerns popularized the anti-hero.

In classic, archetypal storytelling, the maverick anti-hero is the perfect example of the "reluctant hero." He is a man who has no time for saving the fair damsel because he is in the pursuit of riches and power for himself. Han Solo in the science fiction western *Star Wars* is an example of the reluctant hero who ends up saving the day and taking the reward. In the Sergio Leone westerns, Clint Eastwood's character, the Man with No Name (in *A Fistful of Dollars, For a Few Dollars More,* and *The Good, the Bad, and the Ugly*), is the foil for the evil vermin spawned in the American West. In these horse operas, every man is out for himself and the lowest form of life is the bounty hunter. Eastwood's character will sell any bad guy (or even his own mother) for the right price. The conflict in this trilogy is that our anti-hero has an actual human heart beating somewhere under his poncho. His mission is to keep that heart from getting in the way of making a few dollars more. Every one percenter biker can relate to the Man with No Name. The real American West had its share of anti-heroes and many made their way into the history books.

THE PONY EXPRESS

While we have focused on a few of the more famous names of the Old West, there is also a group of men to whom today's biker owes some allegiance. They were the Pony Express riders. Of this group Frank S. Popplewell wrote:

> From the days of ancient Persia to the dawn of modern industry, horse and rider served to bind together the provinces of monarchy, empire and republic. No state long survived its inability to promote the dissemination of knowledge and information among its people. In mid-century America, communication between St. Joseph on the fringe of western settlement and goldmining communities of California challenged the bold and made skeptical the timid. Into this picture rode the Pony Express. In rain and in snow, in sleet and in hail over moonlit prairie, down tortuous mountain path . . . pounding pony feet knitted together the ragged edges of a rising nation. From these hearty souls

who toiled over plain and mountain that understanding might be more generally diffused, a nation spanning a continent was ours to inherit. In the spirit of the Pony Express it is for us to bequeath to those who shall follow, new trails in the sky uniting in thought and in deed.

Pony Express riders were a badass bunch. Most of them were orphans and single young men because the company figured their chances of survival were slim and it didn't want to deal with grieving widows and families. Their ages ranged from 11 to 40 years old and they had to weigh less than 125 pounds in order to make the horse's job easier.

Founded in April, 1860 by Russell, Majors, and Waddell, the company of Central Overland California and Pike's Peak Express Company operated the Pony Express. There were between 80 and 100 Pony Express riders in the mid nineteenth century, and they each rode between 75 and 100 miles before handing their precious mail off to the next rider. On average, they made $100 per month. Express riders favored Mustangs and Morgans for their horses and they changed them every 10 to 15 miles. On average, their riding speed was 10 miles per hour.

The Pony Express rode 1,966 miles from St. Joseph, Missouri, to Sacramento, California, through the states of Kansas, Nebraska, Colorado, Wyoming, Utah, Nevada, and California. It generally took them 10 days to complete their route, unless robbers, rattlesnakes, or Indians stopped them first. This dangerous job was practically a guarantee that its riders would live a hard and short life. But it was technology that truly killed the Pony Express, as these proud and tough men were quickly replaced by the telegraph in October 1861.

Famous biker artist David Mann created *Ghostrider*, perhaps his most popular painting, as a center spread for *Easyriders* magazine (November 1983). *Ghostrider* features a spectral Pony Express rider riding beside a wild and free biker with tattooed arms on his faithful rigid-framed Shovelhead down a stretch of desert highway. The message is clear: the spirit of the biker and the Wild West rider are one and the same.

We have seen so far that whenever there are vast expanses of land or sea, mankind has ventured forth to conquer these untamed wild places. The men who dare to do the taming are generally pretty wild themselves. In every case, we have also seen that as the wilderness becomes tamed, society crowds in to make these wild places civilized and therefore destroys the very

This photo could have been the inspiration for a David Mann painting seen in Easyriders *magazine.*

spirit of the pioneers who paved the way. As the edges of the map are drawn in and the great frontiers grow borders, we see the demise of the Viking, the pirates, the cowboy, and the outlaws.

BIRTH OF THE "MURDERCYCLE"

The end of the Wild West era found America embroiled in great change. Much of this change came about due to the creation of amazing new inventions. Americans began to trade in their horses for new mechanical iron horses. The turn of the twentieth century was a time of wonder, a time when man could dare absolutely anything with the use of machines. Mankind had invented ships that could dive underwater, hot air balloons that could fly through the air, and railroad trains that could steam across the country; new inventions could take a man anywhere he wanted to go.

In 1884, Philadelphia resident Lucius D. Copeland came out with a steam-powered bicycle, but steam had serious limitations on a small, two-wheeled vehicle. Riding a motorcycle is challenging enough without having to shovel coal into the engine, and if you think the rear cylinder on a modern Harley generates a lot of heat on a summer day, imagine wrapping your legs around a functioning boiler.

The gasoline-powered two-wheeler, the conveyance of choice for the outlaw biker, was born in 1885. As the story goes, Mrs. Daimler was out of town and out of mind when Gottlieb Daimler persuaded his teenaged son to take the first test ride on the powered hobby horse that is now considered the first gasoline-powered motorcycle. Unfortunately, Mrs. Daimler came home early, just in time to see her son come smoking and wobbling down the road on the contraption of her husband's design. She was so angry with her son and husband that they did not dare to make another test run for nearly a month.

The Daimler two-wheeler was never meant for public consumption. Herr Daimler built his vehicle, commonly called the *Einspur*, which means "single-tracked vehicle" (though when Daimler registered his contraption with the authorities on August 29, 1885, he called it a *Reitwagen*, or "riding wagon"), solely for the purpose of testing the new gasoline-powered internal-combustion engine. He and his partner Wilhelm Maybach had invented a 26-cc powerhouse that generated 1/2 horsepower. As paltry as that number seems today, when we can go online and order any number of big-inch

"He wore black denim trousers and motorcycle boots and a black leather jacket with an eagle on the back. He had a hopped-up 'cicle that took off like a gun. That fool was the terror of Highway 101." —From the 1950s hit song Black Denim Trousers and Motorcycle Boots

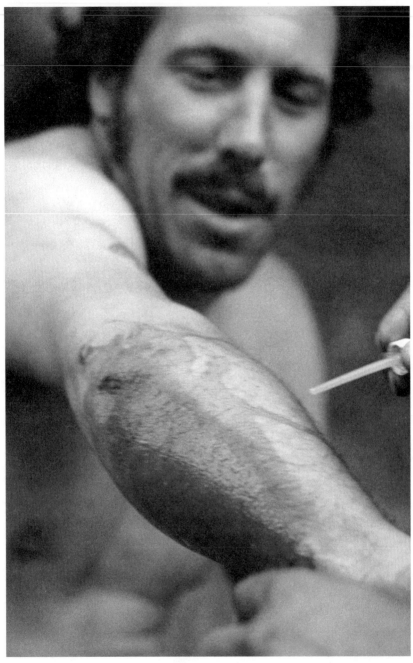

Road rash isn't pretty. Now you know why bikers wear sinister black leather jackets—to save their skin.

150-plus-horsepower, turbocharged, nitrous-injected V-twin engines, the 1/2-horse Daimler-Maybach engine was 1/2-horsepower more than the engines available to any other cyclist at the time. This was a day when cycles were powered by the riders' legs and nothing more.

But a percentage of cyclists wanted more than pedal power, and other inventors followed in Herr Daimler's footsteps and developed gasoline engines that could be used to power bicycles. As these experiments became more sophisticated, several entrepreneurs developed motorized bicycles to sell to the public. Officially, the first production motorized two-wheeler came out in 1894. Called a Hildebrand and Wolfmüller, it was built in small numbers in Germany and France until the company went out of business in 1897. The failure of the venture occurred as a result of the overall design of the machine, particularly its drive system. The engine, a water-cooled twin-cylinder that displaced 1488 cc, was powerful enough, but it transmitted its power to the rear wheels via a pair of exposed pistons in much the same way as a locomotive transmitted power from its steam engines to its drive wheels.

The failure of the Hildebrand and Wolfmüller did not in any way reflect a lack of interest for a motorized two-wheeler on the part of the buying public, and people began to experiment with building their own motorized bicycles. Almost overnight, American manufacturers, such as E. R. Thomas Company, were selling internal-combustion gasoline engines, which customers could strap to their bikes, from the French firm of De Dion Bouton. Into this steaming caldron of innovation came a man named George Hendee of Connecticut.

Hendee raced bicycles in high school, winning 302 of the 309 races he entered. Hendee became a bicycle sales rep, then a dealer, and then a partner in a bike factory. He eventually started the Hendee Manufacturing Company and built his Silver King bicycles. George partnered with Swedish-born Oscar Hedstrom, also a skilled bike rider and builder. They began manufacturing racing bicycles, Hedstrom acting as draftsman and builder, Hendee handling sales and marketing. Their new goal was to build the world's best motorized bike. In 1901, they unveiled their single-cylinder, 13-ci "motocycle." By June of that year, the Indian Motorcycle Company was born.

At just about the same time, childhood friends William Harley and Arthur Davidson planned a motorized bike of their own. Harley worked as an apprentice draftsman; Davidson was a pattern maker. They were into hunting, fishing, and riding bicycles, and both shared a passion for building things.

On many a cold Milwaukee night, the young men found themselves tinkering with small, gas-powered engines. In fact, one of their friends was Ole Evinrude, who would later develop the outboard motor for boating. In the fall of 1900, William and Arthur began producing parts for motorized bicycles using the general design of the popular De Dion Bouton engine.

Arthur Davidson's brother, Walter, was a machinist and helped them put the prototype bike together. At the time, the men were just playing with an idea; they had no intention of creating America's most enduring name in motorcycles. In 1903, the Harley-Davidson Motor Company produced a grand total of three motorcycles out of a tiny 10- by 15-foot shed behind the family home.

That year was a watershed for transportation. Henry Ford incorporated the Ford Motor Company, and the Wright Brothers took to the air in Kitty Hawk, North Carolina, for mankind's first powered flight. With the advent of other famous motorcycle marques of the period—Excelsior in 1907, Pierce with its inline four-cylinder engine in 1909, the Flying Merkel, and Emblem, both also in 1909—America was clearly a nation on the move.

The rivalry between Indian and Harley-Davidson started early on. Hendee and Hedstrom were older men and had more business acumen. To help catch up, William Harley quit his job and enrolled in college to become a much-needed engineer for H-D. Arthur's older brother, William Davidson, joined the Motor Company in 1907 when the partners incorporated. Motorcycling soon took the world by storm, and between the turn of the twentieth century and the onset of World War II, there were literally hundreds of motorcycle manufacturers in the United States.

The long list of American manufacturers gets considerably shorter when you realize how most motorcycles were born in those days. For instance, a company such as Indian might have had proven designers and running prototypes but no foundry or plant to produce its bikes, while big equipment manufacturers such as the Aurora Automatic Machinery Company had the equipment but no design to produce. It was fairly common practice for the latter type companies to make engines for Indian and Pope, in return for use of design improvements for their own motorcycles. (Aurora went on to manufacturer the Thor motorcycle.) That's why Thor motors were used in Pope motorcycles and the combined distribution company produced nearly identical motorcycles with names like Columbia, Cleveland, Monarch, and Imperial.

By the early 1900s, bicycles with motors attached to them made way for true motorcycles. In 1908 Harley built 450 Silent Grey Fellows, as its Model-4,

*Little did Harley and Davidson know that their machines would someday become the
transportation of choice for the one percenter.*

You can bet that Harley oil flows in these boys' veins. The star-spangled number one Harley logo was big in the 1970s ... and so was Aerosmith.

439.9-cc F-head single was called. By the way, the retail price for one of these was $210 when a new Ford was about $300. As any American will tell you, more power is seen as a good thing, and in 1909 Harley doubled the size of its motor by adding a cylinder to create its first 45-degree V-twin 5D model. The new motor displaced 61 ci and produced 7 horsepower. Top speed was a dizzying 60 miles per hour, at least when the thing ran, which wasn't often. The engine used atmospheric pressure to open and close the exhaust valves, a system that worked well enough on the singles, but was wholly insufficient for the twins. Harley produced 27 of the twin models that year, most of which were recalled. It would take the advent of mechanically actuated exhaust valves to make the V-twin a viable engine design for the Motor Company.

Excelsior produced a 1,000-cc V-twin in 1911, which was the same year that Ignaz Schwinn purchased the Chicago-based company. Detroit-based Henderson motorcycles built four-cylinder bikes from 1911 to 1917 when the Henderson brothers sold out to Schwinn, who added the Henderson fours to his line-up of Excelsior V-twins. Schwinn's vision brought Excelsior-Henderson to the forefront of motorcycling and soon, Excelsior-Henderson, Harley-Davidson, and Indian became known as the "big three" of American motorcycle brands.

Advancements and achievements came at a dizzying pace during the early years of the American motorcycle industry. Schwinn built the world's largest motorcycle manufacturing facility of its day in 1914. The six-story building was one of the first all-concrete structures of its kind and featured a test track on the roof. Lee Hunistron became the first daredevil to ride his stock Excelsior past the 100-mile-per-hour mark in 1912. A year later, Carl Stearns Clancy, riding his Henderson four-cylinder bike, became the first man to circle the globe aboard a motorized two-wheeler.

In 1913, Indian developed a form of rear suspension for its Hendee Special, known as the "cradle spring frame," then developed a practical electric lighting system for its 1914 models. Unfortunately, the linkage of the springs and swingarm on the Indian tended to get loose and would wobble easily, while the batteries on the bikes ran down constantly, rendering both advancements useless or worse. These engineering lapses drove more than a few prospective buyers to Harley-Davidson. Worse for Indian, the company's investors didn't understand why Hendee and Hedstrom kept spending money to design innovative products. Ultimately, the original founders had enough, sold their interest in the company, and retired.

Within a few years, Harley-Davidson, Excelsior, and Indian were competing and winning races on the dirt and on perilous board tracks around the world. It was cool to be a rebellious daredevil with smokin' wheels, even back in the early teens. The rivalry among the big three, both on the track and off, continued to burn brightly. In 1914, Bill Harley established the H-D Racing Department and before the year was out, Harley had captured 26 major wins.

Harley-Davidson and Indian motorcycles saw their first active military duty in 1916 in border skirmishes with none other than Pancho Villa. American General John "Black Jack" Pershing and his troops chased Villa back and forth across the border aboard Pershing's fleet of Harleys. Meanwhile, Villa was photographed on an Indian. Guess which manufacturer won the propaganda war among the American public when that photo hit the newspapers?

But the tables turned when Harley and Indian were ready to do their part in Europe during World War I. Some 20,000 Harley-Davidsons were dispatched for scout duty in 1917–1918. In fact, the first Yankee to enter Germany at the end of World War I rode in on a Harley. But while H-D agreed to provide bikes to the military, it also kept its production of civilian motorcycles going. Indian management went all out to provide bikes for the war effort, selling 50,000 motorcycles directly to the U.S. government. Many say that Indian won that war, but its absence from the American marketplace opened up an opportunity that the Motor Company exploited to usurp Indian's crown as the largest American motorcycle manufacturer.

Designer Charles Franklin came on board with Indian and created one of the great little bikes of all time, the Indian Scout, first offered in 1920. The 600-cc V-twin was an instant hit and every boy wanted one. At the time, Harley had nothing that could compare. Still, Harley was tearing up the boards on the racetracks with a first-ever bike race where speeds exceeded 100 miles per hour. Then in 1922, Harley came out with its first 74-ci V-twins, the FD and JD models. Excelsior shocked the racing world in 1920 with a 62-ci V-twin and then really made history in 1925 with the introduction of the famous 45-ci Super X. Indian countered with the Scout 45 in 1927, and in 1929 Harley had a big hit with the WL 45-ci side-valve twin. Unfortunately for everyone in the motorcycling game, 1929 also brought the beginning of the Great Depression.

It was a dark time for America and dozens of motorcycle manufacturers went out of business overnight. Motorcycling had evolved into a recreational activity and there was little money in those days for leisure pursuits. Industry-wide sales dropped from 32,000 cycles a year to a low of just 3,000 by 1933. Major brands, such as the popular Cleveland, went out of business. Even the mighty Excelsior closed its doors in 1931. Over at the Indian camp, wealthy businessman, owner of DuPont Motors, and investor in Indian, E. Paul duPont took more of a hand in running the company. Had it not been for duPont, Indian may have very well gone the way of Excelsior before the Depression was over. As more and more bike companies fell, the remaining "big two" were poised to go to war over which would become top dog on the American motorcycle hill.

In Europe, another sort of war was brewing, one that would eventually produce the latest in a series of rebellious tribes. Unlike the fierce horsemen of centuries past, these bad boys would use cut-up and bobbed Harley-Davidsons to strike terror in the hearts of the straight world.

CHAPTER 3

𝔅irtɥ of tɥe
©ne ℭercenter

THE HISTORY OF OUTCAST AMERICAN VETERANS OF
WORLD WAR II AND THEIR EVOLUTION INTO THE
AMERICAN OUTLAW BIKER.

"What are you rebelling against?"

"Whaddaya got?"

—MARLON BRANDO AS JOHNNY, *THE WILD ONE*

O ut of nearly 300 American motorcycle companies formed during the early decades of the century, by 1934 only two remained in business— Harley-Davidson and Indian. At the depth of the Great Depression, Harley-Davidson pulled out all the stops to stay alive. Luckily, it continued to sell motorcycles to police departments across the country. It also went out on a limb to produce bikes that were more attractive to the leisure market. It got rid of their olive drab paint schemes in favor of two- and three-tone paint jobs with Art Deco graphics.

For the 1930s, Harley came out with such innovations as interchangeable wheels, four-cam valves, high-compression aluminum pistons, a steering head anti-theft lock, buddy saddle, fork spring dampener, instrument lights, and still more power with the creation of the 80-ci side-valve twin. It also introduced the 61-ci overhead valve twin (known by Harley lovers as the Knucklehead), which delivered twice the ponies as the old 61.

Over at the Indian camp Mr. duPont, the new president, fought for the survival of the company and did an amazing job. In fact, each year after 1929 saw the deficit at Indian reduced by as much as half. It cut back and carried on as best it could, putting time and energy into developing the Ace/Henderson-designed straight-four engine for the 1936 model, which basically flopped though police departments seemed to like it. In 1934, the American Motorcyclist Association (AMA) created a new Class C in racing for 750-cc, or 45-ci, side-valve engines. This quickly gave birth to the Indian Sport Scout and the Harley RLDR. In 1935, Harley had Joe Petrali (of Excelsior racing fame) on its Factory Team and Smokin' Joe won *all* of the national titles that year.

Another major victory for Harley-Davidson loomed over the darkening horizon—an upcoming world war. Since the late 1930s, the U.S. government had been giving Indian and Harley ever-growing orders for military motorcycles. These bikes were for war preparedness at home and for our allies overseas, since the British motorcycle industry had been all but destroyed by the German air campaign.

As America entered the war, so did Harley-Davidson, and it entered in a big way. In 1941 literally all of Harley's motorcycle production went to the war effort. The company created the military workhorse known as the 45-WLA, as well as the XA with its horizontally opposed engine, and shipped over 90,000 units overseas. In fact, Harley-Davidson actually received medals of valor from the U.S. Army for meritorious service during the war years. The Motor Company was presented with the prestigious Army-Navy "E" Award for exceptional performance beyond the normal execution of duty in the production of war materials. Indian lost the government bid when it offered a 500-cc Junior Scout. Indian sold many of these to the British government, but for Indian the war of competition with Harley over military bikes was over.

When World War II ended in 1945, motorcyclists stateside wanted new Harleys to replace the ones that carried them through the war years, and returning GIs were aching to buy civilian versions of the military bikes that saved their asses time and time again in Europe. This created a loyalty to Harley-Davidson that Indian couldn't touch. It also gave birth to more than a little rivalry between Indian and Harley riders. When postwar production resumed in 1945, Indian only built its Chief model.

In this immediate postwar period, the rebellious spirit, the warrior spirit, the breed that does not submit to oppression or a quiet life of mediocrity,

As long as there have been motorcycles, there have been those who have cut them apart and customized them.

entered its nexus with the motorcycle—after centuries aboard ships and horse-back. This same strain of rebel had just returned, victorious, from an epic struggle against a mighty enemy. He was ready to shake off the horrors of war and get on with unbridled enjoyment of life in a vast, free country. Some of these tough, independent spirits joined together to form motorcycle clubs, throwing fuel on the legend of the outlaw biker.

In 1930 Howard Hughes made a war film about flying aces in combat called *Hell's Angels*. The name came from a Scottish warrior clan and was adopted by World War I flyers. A motorcycle club in Detroit adopted the name as well in 1938. At this point, motorcycle clubs were fairly clean-living groups who rode while wearing dapper ties and snappy caps. In fact, you could be fined for forgetting to wear your tie to a field meet. The Detroit Hell's Angels even won the AMA award for safety. These forerunners are no relation to today's Hells Angels (note that the notorious bike club we are all familiar with does not use an apostrophe in its name). The one percenters of Hollywood biker movie fame weren't on the scene . . . yet.

The options for these emerging bike clubs when it came to selecting motorcycles were quickly narrowing to one brand: Harley-Davidson. Indian fought valiantly, introducing its new Arrow and Scout models in 1948, but not even Indian-riding celebrities like Jane Russell and Roy Rogers could help Indian when Harley came out with its new 74-ci Panhead motor in 1948. The innovative design featured hydraulic valve lifters and aluminum heads. Harley also unleashed its 125-cc single-cylinder two-stroke model in 1947, the first of a long line of postwar lightweights. In 1948, Harley racers accounted for 19 of 23 National Championship races. In 1949 Harley introduced the classic Hydra-Glide with hydraulic front forks. It was the perfect bike to bob for racing and just the right ride for American servicemen who returned from World War II with a definite need for speed.

Increasingly the new breed of rider was turning to fast motorcycles to try to re-create the excitement he had become addicted to when fighting in Europe and Asia during the war. One such group of speed-crazed World War II vets unwittingly turned the motorcycle world on its head. In the summer of 1946, a handful of American war veterans and their friends were sitting in the All American Bar in South Central Los Angeles, California. The tiny dive was an old gas station with a bar attached in back. Most of the guys hanging out had two things in common: they had been through the war and they loved to race around on motorcycles. The "Big A," as patrons called the place, was a destination for bikers—if you weren't a vet or into bikes, you had no business there.

Some of these guys had been riding motorcycles together since 1939, calling themselves the Characters. Well, "Wino" Willie Forkner, J. D. Cameron and his brother Jim, Jack Lilly, and a few others were knocking back several cold ones and trying to come up with a name for their group of riders. Willie had been thrown out of another motorcycle club for getting drunk and sneaking into an AMA sanctioned race, causing a scene.

As the legend goes, one of the bar's patrons, one Walt Porter, was sitting very drunk with his head on the bar, half-listening to all the talk about names for a new bike club. He is said to have raised up his head and uttered, "You might as well call yourselves the Boozefighters, 'cause all you ever do is sit around the bar and fight that booze." The name stuck and the Boozefighters Motorcycle Club was born. Certainly many motorcycle clubs had come before, but the original Boozefighters and those clubs that came after it marked a change in the evolution of motorcycling because they helped create the concept of the outlaw biker.

When you think of the image of an outlaw biker today, it is almost synonymous with a one percenter (we'll explain how that term came about soon). When most people hear the word "outlaw," they think of a gorilla stuffed into a leather jacket holding a length of motorcycle chain as a weapon or a Wild West gunslinger. The fact is, the term "outlaw biker" referred to those who did not race at AMA sanctioned field meets. Simple as that. These guys would chop everything they could off of Harley dressers to make the bikes lighter. Off went the windshields, saddlebags, and front fenders. They would cut off, or "bob," the back fender and these custom "bobbers" became the forerunners to the choppers of the 1960s and 1970s. These AMA-dubbed "outlaws" were guys from clubs like the Boozefighters, Galloping Gooses, Jackrabbits, and the 13 Rebels. They were outside the convention of the AMA's rules and regulations and were therefore "bad boys."

The human animal of the 1940s was a very different breed from what we are today, both socially and spiritually. Men returning from World War II were combat-tested veterans—hard men with calloused hands who had learned to do what was necessary to survive. War was dirty business and returning servicemen had seen their share of the horrors associated with it. Yet unlike veterans of the later Korean or Vietnam wars, these vets came

Perfect examples of the evolution from bobber to chopper. The Panhead in the foreground still belongs to photographer Kim Peterson.

home to ticker-tape parades, handshakes, and kisses—not that it helped them deal with the inner demons they faced once back home.

The 1940s male was a very different cat from today's "metrosexual" males who swish around in their sanitary office cubicles with a cell phone in one manicured hand and a latte in the other. Men were real men 50 or more years ago and they sought retribution with their fists rather than their lawyers, and they sure as hell didn't share tears with gal pals. The adage, "spare the rod and spoil the child" was still in effect. People beat their kids and men got into fights with bare knuckles if they were called liars or cheats. Americans were made of tougher stuff than they are today. Cowards pulled knives; men used their fists. It was not a kinder, gentler time.

Returning World War II servicemen didn't talk much about the horrors they had witnessed in Europe because a man (and especially a biker) was taught to hold his mud back then. There was no sniveling allowed. Vets kept their demons to themselves and managed to keep their anger on a short leash most of the time.

It was easy for a vet to feel like he didn't fit into the sanitary, Disneyesque world of postwar America. Many felt a lot more at home in the company of other like-minded brothers, hunkered over beers in shitty little bars like the Big A. For the vets in the Boozefighters and other motorcycle clubs such as the Sharks and the Yellow Jackets (the racing arm of the Boozefighters), riding and racing motorcycles and raising a little hell were fun, and fun was what they were about. When you think of the media's portrait of an outlaw biker, you might imagine a group of organized thugs in leather—sort of a chopper riding mafia that deals in drugs, guns, and prostitutes. The motorcycle clubs of the 1940s and 1950s were the opposite of that. These were fun-loving guys who were out to taste a little of the freedom they had fought so hard to win during the war.

In his excellent book on the Boozefighters (*The Original Wild Ones*, Motorbooks: 2005), author and biker Bill Hayes mentions a letter dated September 18, 1946, from Benny "Kokomo" Mitchell, the president of the San Francisco chapter of the Boozefighters, to the Los Angeles chapter. The letter was a request for four club sweaters for new members that had successfully passed the seven "tests" required of a prospect (a prospective member on probation) who wished to become a righteous full-fledged member of the club. These seven tests were as follows:

1. Get drunk at a race meet or cycle dance.
2. Throw lemon pies in each other's face.
3. Bring out a douche bag where it will embarrass all the women (then drink wine out of it).
4. Get down and lie on the dance floor.
5. Wash your socks in a coffee urn.
6. Eat live goldfish.
7. Then, when blind drunk, trust me [Kokomo] to shoot beer bottles off of your head with my .22.

Obviously, these were guys with a great sense of humor and more than their fair share of mischief, but criminals out to rape your daughters and take over small towns for a weekend of violent debauchery? No. The original wild ones were wild at heart but not out to become the next incarnation of the Huns, Mongols, or Vikings of old. Many had served their country proudly in the war. Wino Willie Forkner had been a gunner on a B-52. Dennis "Dink" Burns lost both his legs as his ship went down. Jim Hunter shot down a German dive bomber. Jim Cameron spent his army time in the Pacific Theater. Johnny Davis received a battlefield promotion to second lieutenant for heroic action under fire. "Red Dog" Dahlgren survived Midway. On and on the list goes, but honored veterans or not, these Boozefighters and any other club present were about to fall under a watchful and wary eye of the straight world, thanks to a party that got a little out of hand and a hyperbolic press that dubbed the event "the Hollister Riot."

What happened in Hollister lives in the annals of motorcycling history like some festering sore. The incident single-handedly marred public perceptions of Harley-Davidson and motorcyclists in general. The image of the leather-clad hellion blasting down the road on a loud Harley, out to loot every city, beat every straight citizen, and rape the very flower of American womanhood grew out of some mildly antisocial activities that took place at an AMA Gypsy Tour on July 4, 1947, in Hollister, California. Much has been written about this "occurrence," though little of what the media reported of the Hollister Riot was actually true.

The town had put on motorcycle races long before the alleged riot and had never had any problems with rowdy riders. As the short version of the story goes, an army of bikers came to town riding big chopped Harley-Davidsons (known then and now as "Hogs"), ready to raise a world of hell.

"Hell, we were just getting warmed up." Looks like the Boozefighters have been here.

The perfect bike to chop, a big FLH Harley-Davidson hog.

In reality, it was really just a bunch of bikers having a little fun, but that doesn't make as juicy a story as the one promoted by the press at the time.

Out of the nearly 3,000 riders who came to watch the races and be part of that infamous Hollister rally, the "outlaw" riders amounted to a handful. The misdemeanors that supposedly took place over the course of the weekend were pretty much of the public intoxication or drunk and disorderly variety, with one guy cited for trying to urinate into the radiator of his truck. There was racing in the streets, whooping, hollering, and plenty of drinking, but not anything more outrageous than you would see at a college frat party. About the worst thing that happened was that somebody stole a cop's hat. According to original Boozefighter Gil Armas, someone opened the front door to Johnny's Bar on the main street and said, "Come on in!" Gil rode his bike right up the curb, into the bar, and propped it up against the bar to order a drink (an act which would later be immortalized in the László Benedek film *The Wild One*).

So how did this weekend of shenanigans transform into a riot and turn these fun-loving patriots on wheels into demon bikers from Hell? You have the media to thank for that. *San Francisco Chronicle* photographer Barney Peterson was at the rally looking for a story but needed a catchy image to get his editor's attention. He got an idea and pushed a bunch of empty beer bottles over to a Harley that was parked at the curb. Through careful art direction he created the effect of a drunken orgy, enlisting the help of a rather large inebriated fellow named Eddie Davenport, who just happened to be strolling down the sidewalk. Peterson got Davenport to pose on the bike. It wasn't even his bike, mind you!

The picture and sensationalized story that blew the events at the rally all out of proportion appeared in the July 1947 issue of *Life* magazine and the die was cast. Bikers were the new evil that America was searching for after the demise of Hitler and before the fictitious threat of invasion from space or attack by radioactive mutant insects. Almost overnight, motorcyclists became crazed blood-thirsty bikers in the public's collective conscience. Lock your doors, guard your daughters; outlaw bikers on loud, nasty motorcycles were coming to raid your town!

To combat this new surly image, the AMA issued a now famous press release explaining that the "rough" element of the motorcycling public amounted to only "one percent" of the total riding community. It insinuated that most motorcyclists were good, clean, God-fearing Americans with jobs and families. Naturally, "outlaw clubs" that were sprouting up across the country liked the idea of being the one percent that your momma warned you about and the term "one percenter" was born. Being a one percenter became a proud badge of honor to all those bikers who felt disenfranchised by society. The loners and outsiders now had a name and standard with which they could identify.

As for Hollister, you'd think that the whole thing would have blown over in a few days as soon as the beer bottles were swept up. The public would go back to worrying about rebuilding Europe after the war. In fact, you'd think that the so-called "riot" would only merit a back-page column in the local paper. After all, local citizens who were there on that July 4th weekend had stated time and time again that the whole thing was drastically blown out of proportion. In *The Original Wild Ones*, Bill Hayes quotes a local Hollister woman named Marylou Williams:

> My husband and I owned the Hollister Pharmacy, which was right next door to Johnny's Bar (on the main street). We went upstairs in the Elk's Building to watch the goings-on in the street. I remember that the sidewalks were so crowded that we had to squeeze right along the wall of the building.
>
> Up on the second floor of the Elk's Building, they had some small balconies. They were too small to step out on but you could lean out and get a good view of the street. I brought my kids along. I had two daughters. They were about eight and four at the time. It never occurred to me to be worried about their safety. We saw them (the bikers) riding up and down the street, but that was about all. When the rodeo was in town, the cowboys were as bad.

The incident should have been forgotten as the non-event it was, and it would have been forgotten, had the *Life* photo not stirred the feverish imaginations of creative people across the country. Writer Frank Rooney created a wildly overblown fictional take-off based loosely on the Hollister Riot called "The Cyclists' Raid," which was printed in *Harper's* magazine in 1951. Always ready to cash in on a trend, Hollywood moviemakers saw an incredible new villain in the black leather boogeyman of the type portrayed in "The Cyclists' Raid." Producer Stanley Kramer used Rooney's fictional account of motorized mayhem, along with the events at Hollister, as the basis for his

Being a one percenter became a badge of honor for bikers living outside the bounds of polite society.

1954 film *The Wild One* starring Marlon Brando and Lee Marvin. The film would give the tired old western genre a new twist, with motorcycles taking the place of horses.

Brando rode a Harley in real life, as did his contemporaries Lee Marvin, Clark Gable, Robert Young, Errol Flynn, and Elvis Presley. In the movie, though, Brando's character Johnny putts around on a Triumph while bad boy Lee Marvin gets the chopped Harley bobber. Although Brando as Johnny was the anti-heroic star of the picture, all the real bikers who came to check out the movie in theaters across the country felt a lot closer kinship to Marvin's character, Chino.

While Johnny and his crew of miscreants, known as the Black Rebels, wore fairly clean leathers, black jeans, and boots, Chino and his club, the Beetles, roared into town like a drunken mob on oily, rusty Harleys, dressed like escaped convicts. Interestingly, according to an interview with the late John Lennon, Chino's rowdy motorcycle club's name was the inspiration for the name of the Beatles. The current rock band Black Rebels Motorcycle Club was also, of course, inspired by the film.

From the first roar of motorcycle engines and squeal of rubber during the opening credits, you just know that you are in for a good time. Johnny and his boys are riding into town, having stolen a trophy from the local motorcycle race. The actual bike trophy seen strapped to Brando's handlebars now resides over the mantel in rebel rocker and biker Billy Idol's Hollywood home.

Of course, for straight America in 1954, the year the picture came out, an evening at the movies was more likely spent viewing a light comedy starring Fred McMurray than watching Marlon Brando slur his lines and tear up an innocent town in rebellious juvenile angst. The 79-minute film broke all the traditional Hollywood rules and scared the bejesus out of a lot of people who had a hard time distinguishing between celluloid fantasy and reality. This was really the first biker film and it frightened people enough to ban the picture in the United Kingdom for over 14 years, even though it features no foul language, little violence, and only the vaguest suggestion of sex. What bothered straight society was that the hero of the piece wasn't a hero at all. The thought of a generation of such conflicted and violent young men freaked people right out. Youthful rebellion was not generally something to air like dirty laundry in front of a movie audience at the time.

This bike sports a rare extended girder front end. Bike builder Donnie Smith still makes them to this day.

"Man, this hangover is killing me!" Or maybe this brother didn't want us to reveal his identity.

The movie also had an effect that its producers could not have expected; it created real-life Johnnys and Chinos, bikers who modeled themselves after the characters in the film, emulating their actions and attitudes.

Everyone who rides can cite a defining moment when he or she was bitten by the motorcycle bug. Like many people, one of those defining moments happened to me while I was watching *The Wild One*, which I happened to see on TV when I was nine years old. All that summer I had a "gang" of kids with bicycles in my neighborhood. We would ride our bikes in formation with playing cards making a racket in the spokes. We would pull in front of a neighbor's house and park in a line. After sitting there for a few minutes, I would drawl, "Let's split," in my best Brando impression, and we would ride our bikes to another neighbor's house and park there for awhile. I had been bitten by the two-wheeled bug and I haven't looked back since. *The Wild One* inspired a lot of other people to get their piece of that wild freedom found on two wheels.

At the time the film came out in 1954, motorcyclists either loved it and identified with the bikers portrayed, or they hated the insinuation that all bikers were leather-clad monsters out to sack small towns. Some theaters and drive-ins even considered pulling the film, worried that it might inspire local teens to get rowdy and imitate the on-screen antics of the Black Rebels and Beetles. In fact, newspapers began calling teenage delinquents "Brandos" and police began to harass bikers in an effort to squash any possible biker gang uprisings.

During pre-production, the film's producers signed up Wino Willie to be an on-set consultant. Willie was known for spouting a lot of colorful language and, with all the odd bebop jazz slang in the movie, I always wondered if the writers simply inserted a "daddy-o" every time Willie would have said "sum-bitch."

The Wild One had two lasting effects. It provided a dress code and behavioral textbook for riders who wanted to emulate Brando's swagger, and it firmly planted in straight America's collective mind the notion that bikers were the bad guys. Both effects would linger for a long time to come.

Of course, the Hollister incident wasn't the only bike event in which the media exaggerated mildly reckless behavior to sell newspapers and magazines. The quiet town of Riverside, California, hosted two post-Hollister bike events: one on Labor Day of 1947, and another on July 4, 1948. These two events are often lumped together as wild orgies of street racing, drinking, and fighting, but it was the July 4 whoop-de-do in Riverside that generated the headline: "Cyclists take over town." According to the accompanying article, over 2,000 bikers took over the town and rode wildly in the streets. "With one dead and 54 arrested in the second outbreak of rowdyism from motorcyclists in 11 months," the article claimed, "Sheriff Carl F. Rayburn said he will sponsor no more motorcycle races in Riverside."

Even the local police could not accept this wildly sensational bit of journalism and on July 17, 1948, the Riverside Sheriff's Department released an open letter to the press and public to put the rumors of rowdy bikers and riots in the street to rest. The extent of the damage caused by motorcycle hoodlums that weekend?—an awning got torn down, a bottle was dropped out a hotel window, a man's wallet was stolen, and three motorcycles were stolen, one of which was recovered.

According to Robert Abbott, the under sheriff who wrote the letter, the news media blew the above activity into "a weekend of terror, resulting from an invasion of Riverside by hoodlums and their molls on motorcycles rioting in the streets and wrecking the city." Abbott said that in order to cinch the matter, and to make sure the wire services would carry the story to the entire nation, the news article added the spicy bit that, "the invasion left 49 arrested and one killed."

The under sheriff comments that that one person killed in all of Riverside County that weekend ran into a bridge abutment nearly 100 miles away from the town of Riverside and that the death had nothing whatsoever to do with the rally. As a matter of police record, there were no traffic accidents in the City of Riverside from Saturday afternoon on July 3rd, until Monday afternoon at 1:15 p.m., motorcycle or otherwise. Not a bad record for a township of 50,000 inhabitants.

What of the arrests that the media used to create the illusion of motorized carnage? Here's the list:

Drinking in public: 4 arrested
Drunk: 8 arrested
Drunk driving (motorcycle): 2 arrested
Drunk driving (auto): 1 arrested
Shooting off fireworks: 9 arrested
Disturbing the peace: 12 arrested
Assault and battery: 1 arrested
Failure to disperse: 8 arrested
Interfering with an officer: 1 arrested
Total = 46 arrests

"We want to be free to ride our machines...." —*Peter Fonda in* The Wild Angels

Abbott stated, "To say that the news services have been guilty of gross exaggeration and sensationalism in their presentation of this 4th of July weekend and last Labor Day weekend in Riverside is an understatement." However, the under sheriff did have a warning for alleged outlaw bikers, saying that "The use of streets and highways for drag races and other motorcycle games must be abandoned."

Abbott writes, "Most of the arrests were made in the downtown area while three thousand of the motorcyclists were several miles out of town enjoying clean, healthy games and contests sanctioned by the American Motorcycle Association. It cannot be overlooked that not a single arrest was necessary at the track either day of the races or at the night field meet." Sheriff Abbot went on to offer his sympathy to the thousands of motorcycle dealers across the country which had sent letters or called about the supposed riot, expressing that the dealers' life savings were being affected by the negative press. He also extended his understanding to legitimate motorcycle clubs which had suffered badly from the injustice of the reports.

The letter ends: "In reviewing the evidence developed in this report, one is compelled to acknowledge that the nation-wide sensational publicity given the 4th of July weekend in Riverside, California, was neither honest nor factual—but will in all likelihood hasten the day of a clean name for motorcycling and honest press reporting."

Oh, if only that had come to pass. But, as we all know, the news media is frequently like some rabid pit bull with a toddler when it comes to chewing an angle or story to death. The press had its jaws wrapped around a nice juicy concept and bikers had officially become the bad guys. That press pit bull was not about to let go.

Yes, returning servicemen who fought for America's freedom in the muddy trenches during World War II had come home in search of a little bit of the freedom they fought so hard to win. They found camaraderie in other vets who understood what they were all about. They felt like outsiders as the country entered the squeaky clean 1950s, and their roar of defiance was heard from the straight pipes of their bobbed Harley-Davidsons. But they were not hell-spawned demons on a mission to pillage and burn small town America, nor were they some two-wheeled mafia out to take over organized crime.

One of the earliest bike clubs, the 13 Rebels, had been founded back in the 1920s by a group of movie stuntmen. The Yellow Jackets and Orange

Bet Barney Fife here didn't know he was being flipped off. Oddly, both bikers and cops alike ride Harley-Davidsons.

County Motorcycle Club also rode around Southern California long before the Boozefighters appeared. Other early SoCal clubs included the Rams, Checkers, North Hollywood Crotch Cannibals (there's a happy group), and the Galloping Gooses. In 1949, just two years after the Boozefighters made the scene, a close-knit group of bikers out in San Bernardino started up the Hells Angels.

It's easy to understand why motorcycle clubs cropped up first on the West Coast, particularly in Southern California, where endless summers mean that you can ride your bike every day while much of the country is blanketed in snow. Southern California offers hot rodders and motorcycle customizers the perfect place to push the envelope on design and fabrication. That's also why many custom trends begin on the West Coast and then trickle across the country. In the early 1950s the world of outlaw motorcycle clubs and motorcycle customizing was still in its infancy, but both were about to learn to walk and then run with amazing speed all across the country.

Even in the wake of the media-induced hysteria of the incident in Hollister, Riverside, and *The Wild One*, the Boozefighters and other motorcycle clubs that burned rubber on the highways were still basically "drinking clubs with motorcycle problems." They were fairly tame at the time when compared with what would soon follow. Rebellion and discontent were about to give birth to a very American breed of motorized mavericks.

AMERICAN MOTORCYCLE COMPANIES

MANY CALLED, HARLEY CHOSEN

Approximately 300 American motorcycle and scooter companies have built bikes at one time or another in the United States. The name listed is either the brand name of the bike or the manufacturer. Note how many appeared in 1903 or thereabouts and how many only lasted a few years. Many of these companies lasted less than a single year.

Company	Location	Dates
Ace	Philadelphia, PA	1918–1924
Ace	Blossburg, PA	1925
Ace	Detroit, MI	1926

Company	Location	Dates
Airman	Chicago, IL	1948
AMC	Chicago, IL	1912–1915
America	La Porte, IN	1904–1906
American	Hartford, CT	1904
American	Rahway, NJ	1903
American	Denver, CO	1907–1911
American	Chicago, IL	1911–1914
American	Louisville, KY	1921
American Rocket	Monterey Park, CA	1952
American X	Chicago, IL	1910–1930
Anthony	Colorado Springs, CO	1903
Apache	Denver, CO	1907–1911
Argyle	Memphis, MO	1957–1961
Armac	St. Paul, MN	1905
Arrow	Chicago, IL	1909–1914
Atco	Pittsburg, PA	1912
Austin (steam powered)	Winthrop, MA	1868
Auto-Bi	Buffalo, NY	1903
Autobike	Chicago, IL	1915–1916
Auto Car	Pittsburg, PA	1899–1904
Auto Four	Chicago, IL	1971–1972
Autocycle	Philadelphia, PA	1907
Autocylette	New York, NY	1921
Autoette	Detroit, MI	1911
Autoped	New York, NY	1915–1921
Badger	Milwaukee, WI	1919–1921
Barber	Brooklyn, NY	1900
Barr (steam)	Middletown, MI	1940
Bayley Four	Chicago, IL	1913–1917
Baysdorfer Dumbleton	Omaha, NE	1903
Bean	Boston, MA	1903
Bearcat	Rochester, NY	1950
Beard and Abel	Boston, MA	1903
Bi-Auto-Go	Detroit, MI	1908–1912
Bi-Car	Detroit, MI	1911
Blackhawk	Rock Island, IL	1911–1912

Let this be a lesson to you—Never use your Harley as a barbecue.

Company	Location	Dates
Black Diamond	Philadelphia, PA	1905
Boland	Rahway, NJ	1903
Bonanza	San Jose, CA	1967–1969
Bowman	New York, NY	1905
Bradford	Bradford, PA	1907
Bradley	Philadelphia, PA	1903–1912
Breed	Bay City, MI	1912
Briggs and Stratton	Milwaukee, WI	1919
Buckeye	Columbus, OH	1905
Buffalo	Buffalo, NY	1984
Caille	Detroit, MI	1933–1937
California	Camden, NJ	1906–1908
Camden	Camden, NJ	1906–1908
Centaur	New York, NY	1961
Century	Chicago, IL	1917
Champion	St. Louis, MO	1911–1913
Chicago 400	Chicago, IL	1905
Clark	Torrington, CT	1903
Clemcut	Hartford, CT	1905–1909
Clement	Hartford, CT	1903–1909
Cleveland	Hartford, CT	1902–1904
Cleveland	Cleveland, OH	1915–1929
Clinton Tower	Cleveland, OH	1895
CMC	Gilroy, CA	1997–2001
Columbia	Hartford, CT	1900–1905
Comet	Elwood, IL	1911
Commando	Minneapolis, MN	1950
Copeland (steam)	Phoenix, AZ	1885
Crawford	Hartford, CT	1906
Crescent	Hartford, CT	1906
Crocker	Los Angeles, CA	1933–1942
Crosley	Cincinnati, OH	1943
Crouch	Stoneham, MA	1904
Crown	La Porte, IN	1910
Culp	Columbus, OH	1903
Curtiss	Hammondsport, NY	1902–1912

Company	Location	Dates
Cushman	Lincoln, NE	1936–1957
CVS	Philadelphia, PA	1911
Cyclemobile	Toledo, OH	1917
Cyclemotor	Rochester, NY	1916–1927
Cycle Scoot	Indianapolis, IN	1953–1955
Cyclone	St. Paul, MN	1912–1916
Cyclone	South Gate, CA	1947–1948
DayLake	View, NY	1903
Dayton	Dayton, OH	1911
Delaware	Delaware, OH	1908
Delong	Phoenix, NY	1902
De Luxe	Chicago, IL	1912–1915
Detroit	Detroit, MI	1910
Doodlebug	Webster City, IA	1954–1958
Driver	Philadelphia, PA	1903
Duck	Stockton, CA	1905
Duesenberg	Rockford, IA	1903
Dukelow	Chicago, IL	1913
Dyke	St. Louis, MO	1903–1906
Dynacycle	St. Louis, MO	1949–1953
Eagle	Minneapolis, MN	1909
Eagle	Chicago, IL	1910–1915
Eagle	St. Louis, MO	1911
Economy	Detroit, MI	1908
Elk	Elkhart, IN	1911
Emblem	Angola, NY	1908–1925
Erie	Buffalo, NY	1905–1906
Erie	Hammondsport, NY	1907–1911
Eshelman	Baltimore, MD	1954
Evans	Rochester, NY	1911–1924
Excelsior	Chicago, IL	1908–1931
Excelsior-Henderson	Belle Plaine, MN	1995–2001
Fellbach	Milwaukee, WI	1912–1915
Flanders Four	Pontiac, MI	1911–1914
Fleming	White Plains, NY	1901
Flying Merkel	Pottstown, PA	1910

Company	Location	Dates
F&M	Columbus, OH	1902–1907
Fowler Four	Cleveland, OH	1924
Fowler-Manson-Sherman	Chicago, IL	1905
Francke-Johannsmeyer	Milwaukee, WI	1905
Franklin	Mount Vernon, WA	1899–1900
Geer	St. Louis, MO	1903–1909
Gerhart Four	Harrisburg, PA	1915
Globestar	Joliet, IL	1946–1949
Greyhound	Aurora, IL	1907–1914
Greyhound	Buffalo, NY	1910–1914
Greyhound	Reading, PA	1924
Hampden	Springfield, MA	1903
Harley-Davidson	Milwaukee, WI	Since 1903
Harper	New York, NY	1908
Hartford	Hartford, CT	1907
Hausmann	Milwaukee, WI	1918
Haverford	Philadelphia, PA	1909–1914
Hawthorne	Chicago, IL	1912
Hemingway	Gleenwood, IL	1905
Henderson	Detroit, MI	1912–1916
Henderson	Chicago, IL	1917–1931
Hercules	Hammondsport, NY	1903–1904
Herring	St. Joseph, MO	1899
Herring-Curtiss	Hammondsport, NY	1910
H&H	San Diego, CA	1902–1903
Hilaman	Moorestown, NJ	1906–1912
Holley	Bradford, PA	1902–11
Hudson	Middletown, OH	1910–11
Indian	Springfield, MA	1901–1953
Indian	Gilroy, CA	1999–2003
Industrial	Syracuse, NY	1903
Iver-Johnson	Fitchburg, MA	1907–1915
Jeepette	Los Angeles, CA	1943
Jefferson	Jefferson, WI	1905–1912
Joerns	St. Paul, MN	1910–1916
Kaestner	Chicago, IL	1903

Company	Location	Dates
Kaye-Pennington	Racine, WI	1895
Kenzler-Waverly	Cambridge, WI	1910–1914
Kieffer	Buffalo, NY	1909–1911
Kirkham	Bath, NY	1903
Kokomo	Kokomo, IN	1909–1911
Kulture	Rochester, NY	1909
Landgraf	Chicago, IL	1906
Langford	Denver, CO	1917–1921
La Rey	Milwaukee, WI	1946–1948
Leader	Milwaukee, WI	1906
Leo	Oakland, CA	1905
Lewis	Brooklyn, NY	1901
Liberty	WI, IL and MA	1918
Light Thor-Bred	Pottstown, PA	1901–1908
Lightning	Joliet, IL	1948
Lunford	Marble, NC	1916
Mack	Jefferson, WI	1905–1912
Maltby	Brooklyn, NY	1903
Mansen-Marsh	Brockton, MA	1906
Manson	Chicago, IL	1905–1908
Marathon	Hartford, CT	1910
Marks	San Francisco, CA	1896–1902
Marman	Inglewood, CA	1948
Marsh	Brockton, MA	1899–1905
Maxim	Hartford, CT	1893
Mayo	Pottstown, PA	1903
MB	Buffalo, NY	1903
McDonald	Chicago, IL	1905
Meadowbrook	Hempstead, NY	1905
Mears	Brooklyn, NY	1903
Mecky	Philadelphia, PA	1903
Menns Van Horn	Boston, MA	1903
Merkel	Milwaukee, WI	1902–1909
Merkel	Pottstown, PA	1910
Merkel	Middletown, OH	1911–1922
Merkel	New York, NY	1917–1922

Company	Location	Dates
Metz	Waltham, MA	1903–1906
Michaelson	Minneapolis, MN	1908–1915
Michigan	Detroit, MI	1911
Militaire	Cleveland, OH	1911–1917
Militor	Buffalo, NY	1913–1919
Militor	Springfield, MA	1919
Minneapolis	Minneapolis, MN	1908–1915
Mitchell	Racine, WI	1901–1906
MM	Brockton, MA	1907–1913
Monarch	Hartford, CT	1902–1904
Monarch	Oswego, NY	1912–1915
Monark	Chicago, IL	1950–1955
Mon-Auto	New York, NY	1915–1917
Monnot	Canton, OH	1903
Montgomery-Ward	Chicago, IL	1911–1912
Moore	Indianapolis, IN	1917
Morgan	Brooklyn, NY	1902
Morris-Corkhill	Rochester, NY	1903
Morse-Beauregard	Detroit, MI	1912–1917
Motopede	Rutherford, NJ	1921
Motor Wheel	Springfield, MA	1922
Moto-Scoot	Chicago, IL	1946–1948
Mustang	Glendale, CA	1946–1971
Nelk	Palo Alto, CA	1905–1912
Ner-A-Car	Syracuse, NY	1922–1927
New Era	Dayton, OH	1909–1913
Nioga	Whitney Point, NY	1903
NSU	New York, NY	1908
Nyberg	Chicago, IL	1913
Oakes	Johnstown, PA	1916
OK	Brooklyn, NY	1916
Orient	Waltham, MA	1900–1906
Paramount	Columbus, OH	1917
Parkin-Leflem	Philadelphia, PA	1903
Patee	Indianapolis, IN	1901
Peerless	Boston, MA	1912–1916

Company	Location	Dates
PEM	Jefferson, WI	1905–1912
Pennington	Trenton, NJ	1894
Phoenix	Milwaukee, WI	1906
Pierce	Buffalo, NY	1909
Pioneer	Jersey City, NJ	1903
Pioneer	Worcester, MA	1908–1910
Pirate	Milwaukee, WI	1911–1915
Playboy	Oakland, CA	1956
Pony	Clarkston, MI	1955
Pope	Hartford, CT	1908–1918
Powell	Compton, CA	1939–1952
Pratt Four	Elkhart, IN	1911–1912
Rambler	Hartford, CT	1903–1914
Ranger	Chicago, IL	1938
Razoux	Boston, MA	1903
Regas	Rochester, NY	1900–1902
Reliance	Addison, NY	1904
Reliance	Oswego, NY	1905–1906
Reliance	Elmira, NY	1907–1915
R&H	Brockton, MA	1905
Riotte	New York, NY	1895
Rocket	Columbus, NE	1962
Rollaway	Toledo, OH	1919–1921
Roper (steam)	Roxburg, MA	1869
Royal	New York, NY	1901
Royal	Worcester, MA	1908–1910
Reading-Standard	Reading, PA	1903–1924
Ruggles	Brooklyn, NY	1903
Safticycle	La Crosse, WI	1946–1950
Salisbury	Chicago, IL	1895
Salsbury	Oakland, CA	1936–1942
Salsbury	Pomona, CA	1946–1951
SBM	Brooklyn, NY	1910–1911
Schickel	Stanford, CT	1912–1915
Scout	Detroit, MI	1911
Sears	Chicago, IL	1912–1916

Company	Location	Dates
Shaw	Galesburg, KS	1912
Skootmobile	Chicago, IL	1938
Slattery	Brooklyn, NY	1903
Smith Motor Wheel	Milwaukee, WI	1914–1924
Snell	Toledo, OH	1905
Spacke	Indianapolis, IN	1911–1914
Spiral	New York, NY	1896
Stahl	Philadelphia, PA	1910–1914
Starlin	Tonanwanda, NY	1903
Steffey	Philadelphia, PA	1903–1910
Stormer	Hartford, CT	1907
Suddard	Providence, RI	1905
Super-X	Chicago, IL	1924–1931
Thomas	Buffalo, NY	1907–1908
Thompson	Beverly Farms, MA	1909
Thor	Aurora, IL	1903–1916
Thoroughbred	Reading, PA	1904
Tiger	New York, NY	1909
Tinkham	New Haven, CT	1898–1899
Torpedo	Whiting, IN	1907
Torpedo	Geneseo, IL	1910
Torque	Plainfield, NJ	1946
Tourist	Newark, NJ	1906–1907
Tribune	Hartford, CT	1903–1914
Trimoto	Hartford, CT	1900
Triumph	Chicago, IL	1908–1910
Triumph	Detroit, MI	1912–1913
Twombly	Portland, ME	1895
Vard	Pasadena, CA	1944
Victor	Cleveland, OH	1911
Victory	Plymouth, MN	Since 1998
Wagner	St. Paul, MN	1901–1914
Warwick	Springfield, MA	1903
Wasson	Haverhill, MA	1903
Waverly	Jefferson, WI	1905–1912
Westfield	Westfield, MA	1916–1918

Company	Location	Dates
Westover	Denver, CO	1912–1913
Whipple	Chicago, IL	1903–1905
Whizzer	Los Angeles, CA	1947–1962
Widmayer	New York, NY	1907
Williams	New York, NY	1912–1920
Williamson	Philadelphia, PA	1903
Willis	New York, NY	1903
Wilson	Wichita, KS	1910
Wisconsin Wheel Works	Racine, WI	1903
Woods	Denver, CO	1914
Woods-Meagher	Richmond, VA	1896
Wysecycle	Dayton, OH	1947–1950
Yale-California	Toledo, OH	1902–1915
Yankee	Chicago, IL	1922–1923
Yardman	Jackson, MI	1959
Zimmerman	Cleveland, OH	1950

CHAPTER 4

The Wild Ones

HOW DRINKING CLUBS WITH MOTORCYCLE PROBLEMS
GAVE BIRTH TO THE PUBLIC IMAGE OF VICIOUS
OUTLAW MOTORCYCLE CLUBS. IN A LAND OF SHEEP
A FEW WOLVES STILL ROAM.

Better to reign in Hell than serve in Heaven.
—MILTON, *PARADISE LOST*

Like the well and lesser known rebels of earlier times, literally hundreds and hundreds of outlaw motorcycle clubs have come and gone. Most current clubs belong to mainstream culture, such as the Harley Owners Group, BMW Owners of America, the Blue Knights (police officers), and Wind and Fire MC (firefighters), but we're not concerned with this 99 percent of the riding population. We're only concerned with the one percenters—those riders who fly the one percenter patch.

Dozens of righteous motorcycle clubs, such as the Boozefighters, never wore one percenter patches, but they're still revered by true one percenters because they paved the way on the rough road of bikerdom. A "righteous" club in the motorcycle world is one that stands up for its own. A righteous club member has got your back in any situation. It doesn't matter who is right or wrong in a bar fight. A righteous brother will be there at 3 a.m. when you call him and wake his ass up. A righteous club is "about something," as the biker saying goes. So, a righteous club is a group of brothers who have your back . . . no matter what.

After the AMA estimated that the troublemaking element in motorcy-cling only amounted to one percent of the riding population, it wasn't long before a diamond-shaped "1%" patch began to appear on cut-off denims and leathers. This patch became a badge of honor to those outsiders spurned by society. It was, and is, a proud declaration of a particular point of view, a modern Jolly Roger declaring that no quarter would be taken or given. Bikers wearing a one percenter patch are serious about this shit. Putting on leathers is not a fashion show for these men and riding is not a weekend pastime; it's a way of life.

In the 1950s and 1960s motorcycle clubs sprouted up all across America. This phenomenon had something to do with teenaged rebellion, rock 'n' roll, and the fact that motorcycles are dangerous. Juvenile delinquents saw motor-cycles as a slap in the face for their parents' too-straight world and all its arbi-trary conventions. *The Wild One* helped to foster the image of the modern outlaw biker, and a lot of young guys wanted to be cool like Marlon Brando's Johnny. Plus, girls liked guys who rode bikes. It implied that they were a little bit bad, and as we all know, bad is sexy. It was also a way for girls to freak their parents out. When a greaser with a black leather jacket pulls up on a chopped motorcycle in a hail of smoke and racket to pick up your daughter, you know she's testing her limits and yours.

Motorcycle clubs offer a way for bikers to get together, ride, drink beer, and have a hell of a good time. Clubs are a way to share a common love of motorcycles and also offer safety in numbers to members. In the aftermath of Hollister, Riverside, and *The Wild One*, police agencies across the coun-try started to target anyone on a motorcycle as a bad guy. If you rode a bike, you were suspect. Call it an early form of profiling. Up until the 1980s, if you rode a motorcycle, especially a chopped Harley-Davidson, you might as well have pasted a big sign on your head that shouted, "Pull me over!"

Ask anyone who rode a bike before Harley-Davidson came out with the Evolution motor in the mid-1980s about police harassment. You'll get vari-ations of the same story. Every time you went out for a ride, some cop would pull you over and do a field search. Your bike would be inspected for a bro-ken headlight or taillight, loud pipes, seats that were too low or apehanger handlebars that were too high. The cop would run the bike to see if it was stolen, strip it in search of drugs or weapons, check for warrants and violations, and work the rider over as thoroughly as he did the bike. The protectors of decency spared no effort in providing a bulwark against the Viking invaders.

Outlaw biker or dentist in disguise?

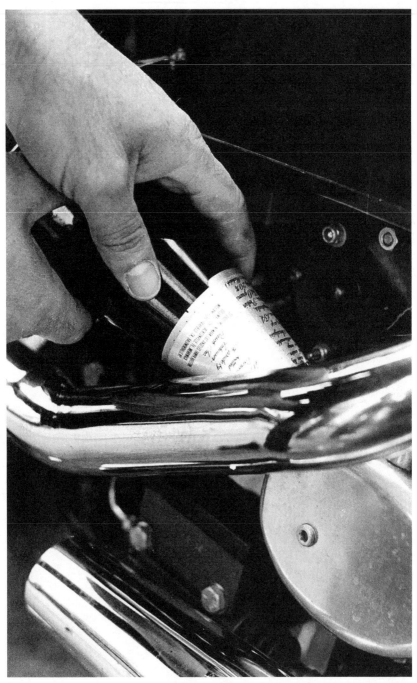

Mini tech tip: Harleys don't drink beer, but beer bottles can be used to add much-needed oil.

One particular memo warned that bikers had a secret device on their bikes that turned their handlebars into shotguns. When a cop would walk up to the motorcycle, the biker apparently would be able to turn the bars in the direction of the officer and shoot him. What a load of bull.

It was common for a lone biker out on the road to be stopped several times during a single afternoon ride. The police seemed to think they were just doing their jobs by keeping the public safe from rampaging two-wheeled monsters. Because of the public perception that all bikers were trash, riders began proudly calling themselves scooter trash or scooter tramps. And cops weren't the only ones giving bikers a hard time. The citizens out there had read the papers and seen the movie. As a result, bikers were refused service at restaurants and not allowed in even the seediest of motels.

There are a couple of scenes in the 1969 film *Easy Rider* that sum up the sentiments of the time. In one, Peter Fonda and Dennis Hopper pull up to a cheapo motel that has a "Vacancy" sign lit up in neon. As soon as the loud choppers pull up, the sign switches to "No Vacancy." The famous diner scene shows how the boys, then joined by Jack Nicholson, are not allowed service and are ridiculed by the locals until they are driven out of the place.

Since the biker image struck fear in the hearts of straight America, bikers were forced to ride together for safety. Motorcycle clubs allowed bikers to congregate and ride together with less fear of getting their asses killed by trigger-happy rednecks. A lone biker was a target; a pack of bikers in a club, riding in formation, was a much more formidable sight. This was one of the reasons that lone bikers joined clubs.

Have you noticed that the taking of small towns and the raping of daughters always seems to crop up? Perhaps it has to do with some primordial human fear of having everything taken from you. Certainly, when you conjure up images of marauding Vikings or pillaging pirates, the sacking and burning of towns and the raping of daughters always comes to mind. Perhaps a part of that fear lies in knowledge of the human race's darkest side, in the way town and city names change and gene pools shift through the centuries as a result of acts that lie closest to our animal nature and farthest from the bounds of law and order. It is this elemental man, dangerous and self-serving, whose image the sheep in society assign to the biker—an image many one percenters embrace.

As was the case with antisocial or anti-establishment tribes of old, outlaw bikers are a rebellious breed, and if the straights wanted to push scooter tramps around, they would be more than happy to push back . . . hard. Public hatred of bikers actually drove the lifestyle to become the antithesis of the straight world harder and faster than anything else could have. If law enforcement and the establishment wanted bikers to be bad boys, one percenters were happy to oblige. In fact, nothing makes a one percenter happier than to freak citizens out. That is one of the reasons for the full open-mouthed "biker kiss" given when two brothers meet each other. The kiss is a genuine display of affection, because brothers genuinely love each other and will die for one another, but its main *raison d'être* is that it sure freaks out Volvo-driving accountants and soccer moms in their mini-vans and SUVs.

So strong is the outlaw biker image, so ingrained in the public consciousness, its presumed attributes spill over to almost all bikers. Put on some leather, hop on a bike, join up with a friend or two, and suddenly you're a potential threat. No doubt in some FBI computer somewhere there is a fairly accurate list of every damned motorcycle club that has ever existed, both mainstream and outlaw. Oddly, the cops seem to have a real hard time figuring out which clubs are one percenter clubs and which are composed of Honda-riding church groups. If you own a motorcycle and wear a leather jacket, you're probably on a list somewhere as a possible terrorist or at least someone who's anti-establishment.

That is particularly funny when you realize that American bikers are among the most fiercely proud and patriotic Americans on the planet. Yes folks, even the members of one percenter motorcycle clubs are loyal, red-white-and-blue Americans. After all, many thousands of bikers proudly and honorably served in World War II, the Korean War, Vietnam, and are now in the Persian Gulf. Having been shot at and maybe fired some shots of their own, their perception of what that means differs from the perception of the guy in a cubicle who wants to sue somebody because he fell on the sidewalk. That right probably doesn't seem as important to one percenters as does the right to twist the grip on a big, loud motorcycle and feel a little of the freedom they bled for.

There is no accurate way to list every outlaw motorcycle club or one percenter club, and this book won't try. Why give the government an easy list to type into its database of "suspects"? Besides, such an effort would no doubt omit some very righteous clubs. Instead we'll focus on the one percenter spirit and influence.

One percenter motorcycle clubs have had an enormous amount to do with how custom bikes, particularly choppers, evolved. No less a motorcycle icon

"I'm so wasted." Another casualty of the biker lifestyle.

"If [these colors] hit the ground even in a fight, I will peel your skin off with a knife dipped in shit!" —Lance Henriksen in Stone Cold

than the Hells Angels' Sonny Barger will tell you that clubs pushed the customizing envelope in creating what we now have come to know as a "chopper."

The bobbers of the 1940s and 1950s started out as stock Harley-Davidsons and Indians that were modified for speed. The idea of bobbing the fenders and chopping up the bike was not for looks or to make a statement; it was all about making the bike lighter and faster. But these early custom bikes evolved to include changes to the stock rigid frame, including the stretch and rake of the neck of the frame. These early customs had no rear suspension, hence the names "rigid" and "hardtail."

Besides chopping the frame so that the bike would have a longer wheelbase for freeway travel, the riding position slowly began to shift from a very upright, stock position to a more laid-back design. This served no useful function, but damn, did it look cool. A laid-back riding position was achieved by taking off the stock floorboards in favor of forward mounted highway pegs. This also necessitated the stock seat to make way for a minimal saddle to be attached directly to the frame and "pullback" handlebars to reach the rider's hands. The frames were often stretched at the backbone so that the gas tank would rise up a few inches. This gave the rider the feeling of sitting down in the bike rather than riding up on top of it.

Passenger seats soon evolved into the classic "king and queen" seats of the 1960s and 1970s, and usually included backrests, or "sissy bars," for passenger comfort, making it harder for your ol' lady to fall off the scoot when she was loaded. The big Fat Bob gas tanks were stripped off in favor of sleek looking Sportster tanks, and early customizers began fooling around with custom paint and more chrome.

Chopping and customizing your bike was a personal statement. Back in the 1960s there were no aftermarket companies from which to buy custom parts. If you wanted an extended Springer front end on your ride, you had to take two stock Harley Springers, cut them up, and weld up a new longer one. The more you extended the front end, the more rake you had to give the frame. Back in the day, no self-respecting biker felt he had the right to ride a chopper that he and his brothers didn't build themselves. No one would ever think of *buying* a chopper from someone else back then. You built your own chopper and knew every nut and bolt on it. A biker and his chopper were one, closer than any marriage, tighter than any brotherhood. It was a way of showing true class.

For those outside the fold, or new to it, "showing class" is slang for doing something righteous that will blow the straights' minds away and gain the respect of your brothers. Building a custom chopper shows class. Making your own parts, helping a brother make his, or doing a wild custom paint job shows class. But so does doing a block long wheelie in front of a church that's letting out or doing a big smoky burnout or doughnut in front of your local biker bar. There are a lot of outrageous things that amount to showing class, like giving a brother a big nasty kiss (as mentioned earlier), or standing up on your seat and doing "the crucifix," or surfing your bike down the road like Indian Larry used to do. Hell, the list of things you could do to show class is infinitely long . . . if you have a good imagination.

The favorite platform choice for most choppers was an American-made motorcycle, but it wasn't the only choice. British bikes were thriving in the States in the 1950s with such marquees as Royal-Enfield, BSA, Triumph, and Norton. These small, lightweight bikes were perfect machines for rebellious teens to do their best James Dean impressions on. Harley counterpunched with its cool little K model in 1952. The 45-ci scoot was the predecessor of the Sportster.

In the 1950s rock 'n' roll was king and, on the cover of the May 1956 issue of Harley's *Enthusiast* magazine, none other than the King himself, Elvis Presley, was seen with his trademark smiling sneer aboard a hip K model Harley. As for Indian, failing sales, a shrinking staff, and uninspiring management put the last nails in the coffin. In 1953 Indian won at the AMA nationals for the last time. On December 2, 1953, a memo from Indian announced to dealers that it would suspend assembly of complete motorcycles at Springfield during 1954, and that was that. Harley-Davidson remained as the one and only manufacturer of American motorcycles.

Harley's new 1957 XL Sportster inspired juvenile delinquents to turn up the collars on their leather jacks, and Harley-Davidson was poised to kick some serious butt. In 1958, they came out with the Competition Hot XLCH Sporty as well as the Duo-Glide FL, and the 125-cc Hummer was added to the lightweight line, replacing the M-125.

The early 1960s brought us *Gidget* movies, *Beach Blanket Bingo*, James Bond, the Beatles, along with the whole British music invasion . . . and a more sinister invasion from the Far East. Having helped set up motorcycling manufacturing plants in Japan in the 1940s, Harley was now being invaded by cheap little scooters and ultra-lightweight imported motorbikes from Honda, Yamaha, Kawasaki, and Suzuki. H-D fought back by making an agreement with Aeronautica Macchi S.p.A. in Varese, Italy. Over the next 18

Back in the 1960s, you built your chopper yourself. No self-respecting biker would have it any other way.

years Harley's model line-up included the Aermacchi line of light and middle-weight bikes ranging from 50 to 350 cc. This included the Topper scooter, the Shortster, the Baja, and, of course, the Sprint. The 1960s also saw Harley producing electric and gas-powered golf carts.

The first year for electric-starters on Harleys was 1965, when the Duo-Glide became the Electra-Glide. This was also the last year of the venerable Panhead motor, making way for the new, improved Shovelhead. Gordon Davidson died in 1967 after a short illness and John Harley soon joined the company. A third generation of Davidsons came to work for H-D as the 1960s came to a close, including John Davidson in sales and William "Willie G." Davidson taking the reins as design director. Harley-Davidson was once again passing into a new era. The privately held company with over 60 years in the motorcycling arena went public in 1965 and merged with the American Machine and Foundry Company (AMF) in 1969.

Competition from Indian was gone, and with its new innovations, Harley-Davidson seemed poised to put many more Americans on two wheels. Yet that one percent of the market, among its most loyal customers, was still posing a quandary for the manufacturer. Public perceptions, fired by an imaginative media, increasingly regarded outlaw bikers as savages on roaring chopped Harleys—the motorcycle of choice for outlaws everywhere. Such notions created a real public relations problem for the Motor Company. Management hoped that Honda's "You meet the nicest people on a Honda" advertising campaign, along with a more wholesome image of scooter-riders, would help Harley-Davidson distance itself from the outlaw image. Harley's print ads changed to squeaky clean portrayals of young, short-haired college kids riding the Aermacchi Sprints and Topper scooters.

Meanwhile, leather-clad American bikers kept buying Harley Shovelheads and chopping them. Even when a rise in motorcycle production caused many new Harleys to have mechanical problems, the bikers stayed true to H-D. It must have been a difficult time for the corporation. No matter what its ads portrayed, the American public equated Harleys with greasy, dirty outlaw bikers, out to invade small towns, rape the women folk, and, well, you know the drill by now.

But how did this violent image spread so fast? Well, bikers had a helping hand once more from the media. In fact, there are many similarities between the Hollister "riot" leading to the making of *The Wild One*, and an incident that led to a more vicious condemnation of bikers in a film called *The Wild Angels*. Once again, the media would "create" its fantasy version based on a real occurrence and exploit it to the max.

This time the fact expanded and exploited for fiction was an infamous incident that occurred during Labor Day weekend back in 1964. Hells Angels and other one percenter clubs from chapters all over California were having a run up to Monterey to raise funds to send a fallen brother's body home for burial. Members of the Oakland chapter of the H. A. (also known as the Red and White for the colors on its patch) roared up through Monterey, right through the middle of town, and parked at a big tavern known as Nick's. By three in the afternoon, over 50 bikes were parked out front, like horses tethered and waiting faithfully before some Wild West saloon.

As the story goes, two girls—one white and pregnant, the other black—and their boyfriends were hanging out and drinking with the club. Local police provided a secluded stretch of beach for the Angels to camp on, and the party eventually moved to the desolate dunes between Monterey Bay and Fort Ord. The cops even posted a guard on the highway to keep the Angels from taking the party back to town.

The so-called "victims" of this encounter later told police that they went to the beach from Nick's because they wanted to see all the cyclists. The two girls and five male friends joined the party around a roaring bonfire. Club members at the scene remember the girls as being wasted when they arrived. Wine flowed, there was talk and laughter, and soon the girls asked to get high. They then walked away from the fire with a few bikers. Apparently, one of the boyfriends got scared and went for the cops.

By early morning, a roadblock sealed the beach and the two women sat in the back of a police car, pointing out which of the bikers present had supposedly raped them. As you can imagine, the newspapers had a field day with this one. California newspaper headlines blasted the Hells Angels for allegedly gang raping two minors (supposedly 14 and 15 years old) repeatedly. What did not make the papers was that medical examiners reported that neither of the girls had actually been raped. Seems like an important omission. Interestingly, the rape case was not first page national news to begin with. Journalists at the time were focusing on the national election story. It wasn't until Attorney General Thomas C. Lynch released a 15-page report condemning outlaw bikers that the national media picked up the torch.

Hitting the road for a weekend party with everything they need … except front brakes.

Within a few months of the incident, major stories by such media giants as *The Saturday Evening Post, Time, Newsweek,* and *The New York Times* helped to create the image of the Hells Angels and other motorcycle clubs as degenerate monsters on wheels. The H.A. went from obscurity to being the major focus of a modern witch hunt in nothing flat. Suddenly, reporters came out of the woodwork to get an interview with a real Angel.

At about the same time, gonzo journalist Hunter S. Thompson was spending a lot of time with the Oakland chapter of the Angels. He would later turn his encounters into an article for *The Nation* (May 17, 1965), called "Motorcycle Gangs: Losers and Outsiders." Thompson chronicled his experiences with the Hells Angels in the book, *Hell's Angels: The Strange and Terrible Saga of the Outlaw Motorcycle Gangs.*

While Thompson's book is a fun read and certainly written in his wonky, whisky-soaked style, the mere fact that the title of the book mentions motor-cycle "gangs" rather than "clubs" shows a skew toward sensationalism. The worst thing you can do is to say that someone is in a motorcycle gang. There is no such thing. Even such infamous one percenter organizations as the Bandidos, Chosen Few, Hells Angels, Hessians, Mongols, Outlaws, Pagans, and Vagos are *motorcycle clubs,* hence the MC on their patches. Got that? There are no gangs.

While Thompson's sensationalized book turned more than a few straight stomachs with its look at the raunchy side of the biker lifestyle, it also was the inspiration for many guys in their teens and 20s to go out and buy a motorcycle. While Thompson's sneak peek inside a one percenter motorcycle club ends on a sour note (the H.A. end up having to thump Hunter a little), the unbridled thrill of jammin' down the highway on a chopped hog sure makes you want to get out on the highway and ride.

Just as with the Hollister and Riverside incidents, the media used the Monterey rape case to sell papers, magazines, and books. In the process, they made the Hells Angels famous. Naturally, with fame comes more fame, or infamy, and it didn't take long for motion picture producers to catch on to the latest exploitable sensation.

The classic movie western had pretty much seen its day by the late 1950s and early 1960s. Moviemakers were looking for something to replace the standard film fare, and after the success of *The Wild One,* they saw bikers as an extension of the outlaws of the Old West. Many a western plot was rewritten, changing out the horses for motorcycles, and a new genre was born: the biker film.

Of all the brilliant low budget moviemakers of this era, two stand above all others: Samuel Z. Arkoff and Roger Corman. Arkoff's American International Pictures (AIP) produced everything from cheesy monster movies such as *I Was a Teenage Werewolf*, to the *Beach Blanket* films and about a dozen low, low budget exploitation films including the now classic *The Wild Angels, Angels from Hell, Devil's Angels, Born Losers*, and others.

Producer/director Roger Corman had worked with Arkoff on AIP's *Attack of the Crab Monsters* and other B-horror movies. In 1966, Hunter Thompson's book, *Hell's Angels* was a hot seller, and it inspired Corman, as did a picture in *Life* magazine that showed a long line of outlaw bikers attending a biker funeral in California for one of their fallen brothers. Corman got together with veteran screenwriter Charles Griffin and, based on that photo and a smattering of information from Thompson's book, created the screenplay for *The Wild Angels*.

Corman was always good at cashing in on trends. He and Arkoff were making movies in a period that was ripe for stories about teenage rebellion, or just plain rebellion. Roger was also able to move fast, make films for very little money, and get them on the screens at drive-ins across the country in nothing flat. *The Wild Angels* tells the story of two members of an outlaw club in Southern California—Peter Fonda as Heavenly Blues (Peter once told me that the name came from drug slang for a kind of morning glory seed that'll get you high) and Bruce Dern as the Loser. The characters played by Fonda and Dern have a hard time keeping regular jobs (they're just too darned rebellious) and eventually decide to go look for some Mexicans that stole the Loser's bike.

The entire motorcycle club, which included actual members of the Venice chapter of the Hells Angels, rides down to Mecca, California, and kicks some ass with assorted motorcycle chains, fists, knives, and blunt instruments. The Loser ends up stealing a cop bike, gets in a chase with motorcycle cops, and gets shot. The club figures that the Loser would be better off partyin' with them than getting much needed care in the hospital and breaks him out of the joint. After some wild, party fun, Dern's character dies and the club, led by Fonda, have to find a place to bury him. First, the members cart him around a lot, stick joints in his mouth, and party with his cadaver.

The highlight of the film is its conclusion in a mountain retreat church where Fonda delivers his famous speech. This has become a sort of biker anthem down through the years. Standing up to the preacher at the church when asked what he and his club of miscreants want, Fonda says, "We want to be free . . . free to ride our machines without being hassled by the Man. And we wanna get loaded!"

Amid cheers from his compadres, a drug-induced orgy breaks out in the church until the cops arrive. The end. Okay, so it's a weirdo plot, but kids across the country ate it up and *The Wild Angels* was heralded as the first real biker movie, spawning a bunch of even cheaper and weirder flicks.

The film's release could not have come at a better time for Arkoff and Corman, since the Hells Angels rape trial was in the news and fresh in the public mind. It also didn't hurt that the film's star, Peter Fonda, was arrested for possession of marijuana at about the time the film was released. As they say, any publicity is good publicity and there was enough of a buzz about the picture that it made over $5 million in its opening month. It was a huge moneymaker for AIP, one of the company's highest grossing pictures of all time.

I remember hearing a rumor that the San Bernardino chapter of the Hells Angels sued AIP for defamation of character after *The Wild Angels* was released and that the club had made death threats to Arkoff and Corman. It seemed that newspapers, magazines, book publishers, television shows, and movie producers were all making a buck off of the H.A., but the club wasn't getting a damned penny for its notoriety. In fact, about all it got for appearing in *The Wild Angels* was a load of beer.

Back in the 1980s I worked at Roger Corman's New World Pictures for a time doing publicity under the guidance of B-movie master Jim Wynorski. Roger was on the set of a silly horror spoof called *Saturday the 14th*, directed by Howard Cohen, and I asked him about the rumor of a "hit" being put out on him by the H.A. Roger just laughed about it. "I remember telling them that if they killed me, they couldn't collect any money. The Angels settled out of court for $2,000."

After Roger Corman's *The Wild Angels* made millions for AIP, a slew of down and dirty biker films spewed out of Hollywood. As always, filmmakers were ready to kick a good horse to death in order to suck every penny out of a new movie genre, and AIP got to work on a dozen different cheesy iron horse operas. Of these films, *Devil's Angels* (1967), staring John Cassavetes, stands out as a particularly revealing foray into the underbelly of bikerdom. In it, director Daniel Haller strings together every outlaw biker cliché then known into a mish-mash of brawls, booze, and badass bikes. The fictitious

MC club, the Skulls, spends a lot of time swilling brew, riding scoots, and apparently have a penchant for demolishing recreational vehicles. The Hells Angels Monterey rape trial was going on when this flick came out, and it was sure to mimic and exploit such perversion with scenes of leering Skulls being accused of raping a whole town full of young ladies.

In classic western tradition, the bad guy bikers are driven out of town by the local lawmen but are then attacked by a bunch of rednecks (a theme common to a lot of biker films). What comes across is some of the *feeling* of being in an outlaw club without any of the substance. The Skulls are seen as a tribe of wandering vagrants who ride their bikes in formation like some guerilla military group, sworn to fun and loyal to none.

Other cheap biker movies followed the success of *Devil's Angels* to drive-ins across the country, films such as *The Glory Stompers, The Rebel Rousers, Born Losers,* and *The Cycle Savages*. Each added to the myth of the modern outlaw biker. In fact, these movies made their way to Europe, where many young bikers used them as templates for one percenter life. The films also added plenty of misconceptions and outright falsehoods.

In the late 1960s, the media circus surrounding outlaw bikers was just beginning. The success of Hunter Thompson's book and the film *The Wild Angels* would only add fuel to the fire. It seemed that the world had a strange fascination with one percenters. Seeing the amazing spectacle of a pack of bikers blasting down the highway on choppers was better than having the circus come to town. Their reported violent tendencies drew the public in like moths to a flame, just as most of us can't help but look at a traffic accident as we pass it, despite the possibility of witnessing gore and death . . . or perhaps because of that very possibility. In a nation of relaxed sheep, there was titillation in seeing the wolf from a distance. But the more publicity that outlaw motorcycle clubs attracted, the more police agencies and government lawmakers took notice.

BEST BIKER FILMS

Of the scores of "chrome pony operas" made between 1954 and the present, the following dozen stand out as noteworthy in the eyes of bikers everywhere. Though most are B-movies to be sure, each offers a bit of that elusive spark in capturing the spirit of the road and the freedom of riding.

Depending on your point of view, these movies comprise the best, or worst, biker films of all time.

1. THE WILD ONE-1953

The movie that started all the ruckus and created a new genre of film is over 50 years old, yet still manages to convey the rebellious spirit of early motorcycle clubs. Though pretty tame by today's standards, *The Wild One* sure stirred things up when it debuted in the 1950s; it was even banned in England. Trivia buffs might like to know the last name of Marlon Brando's character, Johnny. It's only mentioned once in the film: Johnny Stabler.

2. THE WILD ANGELS-1966

"Their credo is Violence—their god is HATE!" The definitive 1960s biker flick. A pre–*Easy Rider* Peter Fonda as Heavenly Blues and Bruce Dern as the Loser lead the ill-fated "Angels" from San Pedro on a series of rumbles and road trips. Tragedy strikes when a rumble gets broken up by the cops and Dern is shot while making his escape on a stolen cop bike. The gang busts him out of the hospital and, of course, he croaks, leading to the most insane drug-soaked funeral orgy of all time.

Made in 1966 by cheapskate genius filmmaker Roger Corman, this is really the flick that launched the biker movie craze. Lots of real bitchin' bikes and riding scenes in this one, and you get to drool over a nubile Nancy Sinatra.

3. HELLS ANGELS ON WHEELS-1967

The opening sequence in this movie presents one of the most powerful visions of the biker world ever captured on film. Jack Nicholson plays Poet, a drifting loner who tangles with, joins, and then quits the Hells Angels. The action that ensues is some of the greasiest fun you could ever see. They fight, they love, and they ride like friggin' maniacs.

4. THE REBEL ROUSERS-1970

Jack Nicholson, Bruce Dern, and Harry Dean Stanton lead their gang into a little desert town for some sociopathic good times. Cameron Mitchell and Diane Ladd are a couple of squares who stumble onto the gang's psycho beach party (this ain't Frankie and Annette) and are taken as prisoners. Nicholson is great as Bunny, the demented loose cannon with the coolest pants in town.

5. SAVAGES FROM HELL-1968

"Their motors are flaming, their mamas are on fire . . . they're dogs on the loose!" Bikers, beach parties, body painting, death by dune buggy, interracial lust, and a good old-fashioned cat fight all gleefully collide in this bit of cycle celluloid. Made by Mexican kiddy horror kingpin K. Gordon Murray and once called "the *Ben-Hur* of biker flicks," this one pits the outlaw bikers against migrant farm workers, with a good-looking babe caught in the middle.

6. EASY RIDER-1969

The ad campaign for *Easy Rider* proclaimed, "A man went looking for America and couldn't find it anywhere." But the movie that became the anthem for the Woodstock generation wasn't just about a couple of drug dealers turned hippy bikers who get blown away by southern rednecks. *Easy Rider* was about getting the easy ride and selling out. The term "easy rider" is southern slang for the boyfriend or husband of a hooker because he gets the easy ride. Throughout the film Peter Fonda's Wyatt and Dennis Hopper's Billy are given chances to settle down and be about something. By the end of the film Fonda has figured out that they are on a road to nowhere and tells Hopper, "We blew it."

Beautiful riding shots by cinematographer László Kovacs, featuring gleaming choppers, set to great rock music, inspired a whole generation to go out, buy a motorcycle, and ride off in search of a little freedom.

7. C. C. AND COMPANY-1970

Football legend Joe Namath teams with Ann-Margaret in this tale of a smooth-talking drifter C. C. Ryder (Namath), who rides with a gang called the Heads. When the gang attacks a New York fashion writer (Margaret), Namath breaks ranks and goes on the lam with Ann, who is a member of his former gang. Yeah, like you wouldn't! Danger, passion, and suspense build with each narrow escape until the final race to settle the score.

8. THE BLACK ANGELS-1970

An epic exercise in bad acting, the flick centers around an ongoing gang war between two cycle mobs, the Choppers (a real Southern California black MC) and Satan's Serpents. Best of all, *The Black Angels* contains one of the best lines in cinema history: "I'm gonna kill you, you no-good egg-suckin', finger-lickin', snot-pickin', scuzzy-faced rat!" Gotta love it.

Is this the man your mother warned you about? Either way you look at it, his ride is sweet.

9. HELLS ANGELS '69-1969

Starring the real Oakland Hells Angels, this casino heist caper is just weird from beginning to end. Jeremy Slate (who wrote the screenplay) and Tom Stern play a couple of bored jet-setters who concoct a truly stupid plan to rob a Las Vegas casino by posing as members of a fake motorcycle gang (the Witches from Salem, Massachusetts). They hook up with the Angels for a few weeks of riding and scheming. The story here is totally retarded. What's cool is the Angels are not really acting but being themselves. And Terry the Tramp *rules*. The final chase scene, well, let me just say . . . *patch holders on dirt bikes.*

10. ANGEL UNCHAINED-1970

Bikers versus townies in defense of hippies. Don Stroud plays Angel, a wandering biker who rides into a small town looking to leave his past behind. He finds compassion from a young Tyne Daly, who lives at a hippie commune just outside of town. The townies, of course, hate the hippies and tear them up relentlessly. Angel recruits the help of his old gang, which then rides in like a freak cavalry to save the day.

11. BORN LOSERS-1967

The movie that introduced the character of Billy Jack to the world. Tom Laughlin plays the aforementioned Billy, a half-breed Indian who single-handedly kicks the living shit out of a bike gang as it plots its reign of terror on small-town America. The gang leader, played by Jeremy Slate, has the goofiest big white sunglasses you ever did see.

12. STONE COLD-1991

This action-packed flick brings the vibe of old biker films into the modern age. Football dude Brian Bosworth plays John Stone, an undercover cop assigned to infiltrate a notorious bike gang led by Chains (Lance Henriksen). Henriksen gives a badass performance, as does William Forsythe as his second in command, Ice. The plot thickens as we learn the gang's plan to rescue a member on trial with a full military assault on the state capital. Check it out. There was a similar movie that came out at about the same time called *Beyond the Law* with Charlie Sheen, but this one is way better.

There are lots of other two-wheeled treats that almost made this Biker Movie List. *Wild Rebels*; *She-Devils on Wheels*; *Run, Angel, Run*; *Chrome and*

Hot Leather; Werewolves on Wheels; and *The Loveless* are all worth a viewing and are available through Whitehorse Press. Also, if you're into the whole cycle cinema thing, read Mike Seate's excellent book, *Two Wheels on Two Reels: A History of Biker Movies,* also available through Whitehorse Press, www.whitehorsepress.com, 800-531-1133.

CHAPTER 5

There Are No Gangs

THE DEPICTION OF OUTLAW BIKERS BY THE MASS
MEDIA: HOW CLUBS BECAME GANGS IN THE PUBLIC
CONSCIOUSNESS AND THE RISE OF THE RICO ACT.

Three can keep a secret if two are dead.
—FAMOUS EXPRESSION OFTEN
ATTRIBUTED TO BENJAMIN FRANKLIN

The evolution of American bikers from tie-wearing Dapper Dans on stock dressers to World War II vets in bomber jackets and black jeans on chopped bobbers didn't happen overnight. The same is true for the gradual change from Boozefighter to Hells Angel. The image of the outlaw biker continued to degrade in the 1960s for several reasons. One was that the media looked for any opportunity to exploit the outlaw image in order to sell newspapers, magazines, and the nightly newscasts. Naturally, the public, being good little sheep, accepted whatever the media told it and was happy to have something new and exciting to hate.

However, another reason for the degradation of bikers came from within bikerdom itself. As we have seen, outlaw bikers in the 1960s fit within the mold of the nonconformist; they were basically anti-establishment and against the squeaky clean image of wholesome *Happy Days* America. Being shunned by straight society encouraged bikers to rebel all the more. They had fun blowing the straights' minds by dressing in grubby originals, letting their hair and beards get long and greasy, and roaring around on loud choppers, raising hell. Outlaw bikers wanted to distance themselves from the straight-laced citizenry, and one way to do that was to become the antithesis of the white shirted, church-going, good guy. Bikers wanted to be bad and became more filthy and outrageous in order to thumb their noses at the straight world and give decent society the finger. One percenters were basically Ozzie and Harriet turned on their heads. If the young Christy Minstrels wanted to sing happy songs about better living through chemistry, the one percenters screamed "fuck the world" (seen as FTW on their cut-offs) and embraced Steppenwolf's "Born to be Wild" as their anthem. The 1960s were a time of sex, drugs and rock 'n' roll, and one percenters wanted as much of all three as they could get their oil-stained hands on.

Marijuana and acid lubricated the path toward more relaxed morals and even longer hair. Many bikers during this time period were basically hippies on motorcycles, but this could not be said of the one percenter motorcycle club members. Clubs were, and are, tight knit organizations with an almost militaristic zeal. Their leaders are frequently charismatic men with strong leadership skills. Many motorcycle clubs become homes to war veterans who are used to military order. Originally Nazi accoutrements entered the motorcycle culture because soldiers-cum-motorcyclists brought them home from the war as souvenirs, but the reason some outlaw bikers wore German World War II iron crosses, swastikas, SS medallions, and even German helmets was because they respected the organization, might, and spirit of the Third Reich. Outlaw bikers may not condone what the Nazis did, but they admire the loyalty and dedication of the organization.

This leads us to the accoutrements of the one percenter. Every patch holder of an outlaw club wears "colors," the proud banner of his organization. It is the flag, church, and brotherhood of the club incarnate. It is the visual statement of who and what they are. As such, a member's club colors are sacred and, like the flag of his country, must never touch the floor, even in a fight. When a prospective member of an outlaw club, known as a prospect, is indoctrinated into the club as a fully patched member, he goes through a simple ritual with his club brothers, which varies in intensity from club to club. This rite of passage brings him officially into the club, and he is then given his club colors. They consist of a cut-off denim jacket with the club's patches sewn on the back. Along with this cut-off, black jeans (black hides motor oil better) become the member's "originals," (his uniform), and he will wear them proudly until they are reduced to rags before replacing them. A real biker's originals are so encrusted in motor oil, road grime, and other crap that they will stand up on their own in the corner.

It's rare to see swastikas being worn anymore; almost as rare as seeing a rider kick-starting a bike.

Who needs a full dresser when you can go get beer on your chopper?

Club colors consist of a top rocker that announces the name of the club and a bottom rocker stating to which chapter the member belongs. In between the two rockers, in the middle of the back of the cut-off is the club's insignia, or patch. The rockers and patch are all displayed in the two prominent colors of the club. For instance, the Hells Angels are red and white, the Bandidos are yellow and orange, the Outlaws are black and white, and the Vagos are red and green. There is a square patch that bears the legend "MC" and, on the front of the cut-off, there is a diamond-shaped patch with the famous "one percent" sign emblazoned on it. Other patches include a number 13, which stands for the 13th letter in the alphabet (the letter M). In time honored outlaw biker tradition, this means the member smokes marijuana. There are also assorted motorcycle run pins that show off the runs on which the member has been, rectangular patches along the bottom front of the cut-off that honor club member brothers who have died ("In memory of," or "RIP"), and there are also sometimes different colored Harley wing patches.

A WORD ABOUT "WINGS"

It used to be that every Harley-Davidson dealership across the country would sell different-sized Harley logos that you could sew on your denim cut-off or leather jacket. Many still do. Bikers favored the Harley bar and shield logo, and many of these also sported a set of bird-like wings sprouting from each side of the bar and shield. The larger version of this logo was often sewn onto the bottom of the back of a jacket. In recent years, some bikers have turned this set of Harley wings upside down as a way to show their disgust with the Motor Company for selling out the loyal customers in favor of good old American greed.

The smaller wings (about 3 inches across) became very famous for a completely different reason. Rather than showing support for the Motor Company, these small wings became badges of dubious honor for outlaw motorcycle clubs. Back in the 1960s and 1970s, homosexuals used to wear different colored bandannas in their rear pockets to let prospective lovers know their sexual preferences: yellow for golden showers, and so on. Well, for one percenters, the small Harley wings were used to tell the world many of their preferences as well . . . though they have nothing, I repeat, *nothing* to do with homosexual practices.

Check the different rake and stretch on these two choppers. The long springer front ends look like those built by Denver's Choppers.

As legend has it, the small red wings were the most famous, or infamous. Though red wings carries the same name of the ancient Viking torture mentioned in Chapter 1, it has nothing to do with that horrific form of death. A prospect "earned" his red wings by going down on a girl while she was having her period. Besides being another great way to screw with the straight citizens' minds, red wings show a macabre sense of humor that is just a cruder, rowdier extension of the antics of early clubs—such as the Boozefighters which asked prospects to "hit another prospect with a lemon pie."

Over the years, the meanings of the other colored wings have changed depending on the club. For instance, some say that black wings mean that you killed someone for the club, others say they mean you like to have anal sex with girls, and still others say it means you've had sex with a black girl. Prison tattoos often have similar secret meanings. Supposedly, it used to be that if you had a spider web tattooed on your elbow, it meant you killed someone for the club. Of course, the police agencies took any and all such rumors to heart, whether it was all just bullshit or not. In fact, many of the memos that have been generated by police departments about what tattoos and club patches mean are hilariously wrong.

Just as completely incorrect have been the media's reports of initiation rites for outlaw clubs. As written about in many books and magazines, and satirized in many biker movies, the prospects have one helluva tough time. An independent biker (someone who doesn't ride with any club) will start hanging around with club members and becomes known as a hang-around. All the members check him out, see what kind of guy he is, and make sure he can ride the snot out of his bike. They may offer him little challenges to see if he's a piece of shit or to find out if he's about something. If he turns out to have true grit and be a righteous biker, they may let him prospect for the club. The biker is then allowed to wear a prospect patch on his cut-off. Generally, a prospect is the bottom man on the bike club totem pole; whatever a patch holder tells the prospect to do, he had better do it . . . and fast. This may include standing outside in the freezing cold and watching all the club members' bikes while the rest of the club is inside a nice warm bar partying. It may include guarding the site of a party or run, it might mean that he hauls his ass to the store a dozen times for beer, and it sure as hell means that no club brother's beer is ever empty.

A prospect is allowed to attend church night (when the club meets once a week to take care of club business) but is not allowed to vote on anything; he's too busy refreshing the patch holders' drinks. Many clubs will kick a prospect out of the club if his bike is down and not operating, or for any infraction, real or imagined. Since the 1980s most clubs are constantly on the alert that prospects might in fact be undercover cops trying to infiltrate their organization to see what criminal activities, if any, they're up to. You have to prove yourself again and again to be a loyal, stout-hearted brother to have any hope of becoming a fully patched member.

Prospecting can take several years in some clubs before a prospect earns his patch. When that happy day comes, a special ritual is held in his honor. This is often a complete surprise to the prospect. Sometimes a club president will even make the prospect think that he is being pitched out before handing over his beloved patch. Myths about this rite of passage have been greatly exaggerated in the media. You'd think that the members of all outlaw biker clubs put on goat legging and drink human blood before letting someone "patch in." In most cases, a prospect getting his patch becomes one big party.

As outlaw motorcyclists became the long-haired, greasy, filthy, disgusting brutes that the media wrote about in order to further fuck with the straight world and flip convention the finger, the police began to target them more and more. At the same time, the straight world began to kick them out of more restaurants, hotels, parks, and even bike runs. While respectable moms and dads saw one percenters as the devil incarnate, college-aged kids saw them as free spirits (a theme that would be exploited in the film *Easy Rider*). Hunter Thompson's book, *Hell's Angels*, did much to focus America's attention on one of its most notorious motorcycle clubs, but in the mid-1960s, there were dozens of one percenter clubs operating across the country. Many of those clubs were giving the media plenty of good reasons to write nasty stuff about them.

Just about every article written over the years added to the general feeling that one percenter clubs were up to no good, but there were many club members who actually enjoyed the negative publicity . . . at first. After all, if the straights wanted them to be bad boys, they were happy to oblige. What were they rebelling against? Waddaya got?

As the one percenters' notoriety grew, police harassment got pretty bad. You couldn't even ride your scoot down to the corner store for a pack of smokes without getting pulled over for any number of bullshit violations. The cop would always say that he was pulling you over because your pipes were too loud or your apehangers were too high, or you had a taillight out.

The truth was, he wanted to run you for warrants, check to see if your chopper was stolen, see if you were high or drunk, check you for weapons, and so on. Since they were happy to be the bad guys, cops were happy to be the good guys and throw them in the slammer.

Now I'm not saying that one percenters are choir boys, but the vast majority of motorcycle club members are also not the murderers and rapists that they have been made out to be either. As with any organization, a club cannot police all its members. If one of the members is stealing bikes or selling drugs, the whole club is blamed. Newspaper articles that cited club members involved in criminal activity always got big press. Some of these stories acted as the fodder for cheapo biker exploitation films.

With all the barbarous acts both real and imagined heating up the media, one percenter clubs became notorious across the land and lawmakers were put on the spot to do something about these degenerate groups of miscreants. In 1970, Congress passed the Racketeer Influenced and Corrupt Organizations (RICO) Act, Title 18, United States Code, Sections 1961–1968. The idea was to curtail organized crime, which was affecting the American economy, and to eliminate the Mothers and Fathers Italian Association, also known as the Mafia. It is interesting to note that in Italian, the word *ricco* means "rich." Some have theorized that the RICO Act got its name from the gangster film, *Little Caesar*, whose lead crime boss was named Rico.

Under the RICO Act, a person or group who commits any 2 of 35 crimes—27 federal crimes and 8 state crimes—within a 10-year period and, in the opinion of the U.S. Attorney bringing the case, has committed those crimes with similar purpose or results, then that person or group can be charged with racketeering. Those found guilty of racketeering can be fined up to $25,000 and/or sentenced to 20 years in prison. In addition, the racketeer must forfeit all ill-gotten gains and interest in any business gained through a pattern of "racketeering activity." The act also contains a civil component that allows plaintiffs to sue for triple damages.

When the U.S. Attorney decides to indict someone under RICO, he has the option of seeking a pre-trial restraining order or injunction to prevent the transfer of potentially forfeitable property, as well as require the defendant to put up a performance bond. This provision is intended to force a defendant to plead guilty before indictment.

What is racketeering? It is defined as any act or threat involving gambling, murder, kidnapping, arson, robbery, bribery, extortion, dealing in obscene

"Why you looking at me? My name ain't Rico."

Harley's Sportster was a perfect platform to build into a chopper. This scoot is a prime example.

matter, or dealing in a controlled substance (that is chargeable under state law and punishable by imprisonment for more than one year). It also includes any act that is indictable under a wide variety of specific provisions of title 18 of the U.S. Code relating to bribery, counterfeiting, theft, embezzlement, fraud, obscene matter, obstruction of justice, slavery, racketeering, gambling, money laundering, commission of murder-for-hire, or the manufacture, importation, receiving, buying or selling of a controlled substance (meaning drugs). There is more—much more—involving illegal labor and trade, bringing in or harboring aliens, and so on.

One of RICO's most successful applications has been to indict or sanction individuals for their behavior and actions committed against witnesses and victims in alleged retaliation or retribution for cooperating with law enforcement or intelligence agencies.

When the court perceives a "pattern of racketeering," it can use the RICO Act to run surveillance on any group that it believes might be guilty of participating in organized crime. Use of the RICO Act has put away crime bosses to be sure, but it has also been used to target motorcycle clubs and street gangs. Any member of a one percenter motorcycle club can be convicted of "conspiracy" and can be thought to be guilty by association with known felons in his organization. Not long after RICO was enacted, there were a lot of club brothers in the pen. This made other club members go into hiding, and the government had effectively put its thumb on one percenter clubs across the country.

To show the kind of lawless behavior targeted by RICO, the following are just a few of the more famous cases:

On November 21, 1980, Frank "Funzi" Tieri was the first Cosa Nostra boss to be convicted under the RICO Act.

In June 1984, the Key West Police Department in Monroe County, Florida, was declared a "criminal enterprise" under the Federal RICO statutes after a lengthy U.S. Department of Justice investigation. Several high-ranking officers of the department, including Deputy Police Chief Raymond Cassamayor, were arrested on federal charges of running a protection racket for illegal cocaine smugglers. At the trial, a witness testified he routinely delivered bags of cocaine to the deputy chief's office at City Hall.

In 2002, former owners of the Montréal Expos baseball team filed charges under the RICO Act against major league baseball commissioner Bud Selig and former Expos owner Jeffrey Loria, claiming that Selig and Loria deliberately conspired to devalue the team for personal benefit in preparation for a move. The case lasted for two years, successfully stalling the Expos' move to Washington.

On August 8, 2006, in Tampa, Florida, over 30 members of the street gang, the Latin Kings, were arrested in connection with RICO conspiracy charges and currently await trial.

On October 16, 2006, four members of the Gambino Crime Family (Terry Scaglione, Ronald Trucchio, Kevin Mcmahon, and Steven Catallono) were tried under RICO statutes, found guilty, and sentenced to life in prison.

Judging by the above examples, it would seem the RICO Act works as intended, and in some instances it probably does. The problem with the RICO Act is that it can be abused. Originally meant to stop organized crime conglomerates such as the Mafia, it has been used to target motorcycle clubs on the pretext that one percenter clubs exist solely to pursue criminal activities. RICO allows police to arrest all the members of a motorcycle club for a crime committed by one of its members. Freedom from guilt by association would seem to be a fundamental right under the law of the United States . . . except that it is not. Under RICO you may be tried for your membership or association with an organization. In an age of the "war on terror," this is a frightening concept.

The Fifth Amendment to the United States Constitution guarantees that a person shall not be tried twice for the same offense. This is known as double jeopardy. But even if you've been tried, convicted, and sentenced for an offense, under RICO you may be tried and convicted again for the very same acts. You can also be tried again after being found not guilty. You may also be tried and convicted for crimes that happened 10 to 15 years ago. There is no statute of limitations or right to a speedy trial under RICO. Welcome to America, land of the free . . . as long as you don't ride a motorcycle, that is.

So, from good-natured drinking clubs with motorcycle problems, the image of the biker in America turned dark. Bikers began to turn up as the bad guys on television shows, taking the place of Wild West outlaws.

Being a biker was no longer a wholesome pursuit according to the mass media. We became the people that your mother warned you about. Just as the die was cast on badass bikers and the stereotype stuck fast, a film about the American dream and freedom became the anthem for the Woodstock generation.

CHAPTER 6

Easyriders

WHEREIN A BIKER LIFESTYLE GAINS MOMENTUM
IN A TIME WHEN AMERICA NEEDED REBELS:
THE PHENOMENON OF THE FILM *EASY RIDER*
AND *EASYRIDERS* MAGAZINE.

"You know Billy, we blew it."

—PETER FONDA, *EASY RIDER*

The turbulent 1960s was a time of war and chaos. Timothy Leary was teaching us to "tune in, turn on, and drop out." We lived through Vietnam, Kent State, Watergate, hippies, yippies, and Woodstock. What a long, strange trip it's been. In fact, one of the legends regarding the "origin" of the one percenter patch comes from the 1960s. In 1961, the AMA had an advertising campaign known as "Put your best wheel forward," which encouraged riders to clean up their act and offer up a clean public appearance. Well, you can imagine how that went over with outlaw bikers. One percenters who scoffed at the AMA campaign began wearing American Outlaws Association (AOA) patches. These eventually became the infamous one percenter diamond patches seen today.

Bad biker movies were a hit at drive-ins in those flower-power days of yore, and certain notorious motorcycle clubs continued to show up in the press, never for doing something nice. While there was a brief time when hippies and acid heads invited Hells Angels to parties in Haight-Ashbury, this came to sudden end when a group of HAs disrupted a peace march in 1965. The Oakland chapter even offered to go to Vietnam and fight as a "crack group of fighting guerillas," but for some reason President Lyndon Johnson declined the offer.

Outside the motorcycle world, the average Joe Citizen still misunderstood what bikers were all about. The press continued to print exaggerated accounts of any and every minor scuffle that included anyone remotely associated with a motorcycle, creating the impression that the entire country was under siege by legions of motorized Visigoths. The so-called Laconia Riot, a non-incident that took place in 1965 at the Loudon Classic Rally and Races in Laconia, New Hampshire, enforced the hyperbolic stories used by the press to sell newspapers and magazines, stoking the fears of the hysterical masses.

At the time of the Laconia incident, the public's attitude toward outlaw bikers had been poisoned by California Attorney General Thomas C. Lynch and his Lynch Report, a 15-page document based on a 10-year study of the Hells Angels and other motorcycle clubs published on March 15, 1965. Newspapers and news magazines used the report as a banner to preach their dim view of all motorcyclists to the public. On May 17, 1965, *The Nation* magazine published Hunter S. Thompson's article, "The Motorcycle Gangs: Losers and Outsiders." The one-two punch of the Lynch Report and Thompson's article set the stage for press coverage of the Laconia incident, also known as the riot that never happened.

The short version of this story is that the 44th running of the annual Loudon Classic took place on June 19 and 20, 1965. Thirty-four motorcyclists were arrested and 70 people were injured. The incident made national headlines, including *Life* magazine's article by Michael Mok. To his credit, Mok was not quick to condemn the bikers in Laconia, citing that crew-cut college kids joined bikers in the supposed riot. He also points out that "brawlers and bystanders alike" were injured by National Guard. While the Hells Angels were blamed for starting the riot, its members denied being anywhere near Laconia. Interestingly, damage from the riot was minimal and the races went on as scheduled the next day. But the public generally links the words "riot" and "Hells Angels," just as it links the words "rape" and "Hells Angels," even though the club was acquitted in the Monterey Rape case because the medical examiner found no evidence that the young women who made the charges had been sexually assaulted.

So far, the red and white had the lion's share of bad publicity. Then, in 1967, the Outlaws MC became the focus of intense media attention. It seems that a chapter of the Outlaws MC in Florida was accused of "crucifying" a pretty young girl named Christine Deese. This caused the state's governor,

Claude Kirk, to declare war on Florida's motorcycle clubs. Newspapers claimed that Christine was nailed to a tree as punishment for not giving all her money to her boyfriend, who happened to be a member of the Outlaws. After a cross-country manhunt, the boyfriend and three other members of the Outlaws MC were captured, booked on aggravated assault charges, and jailed on $15,000 bail.

But all this was just a prelude to an incident that would make major headlines due to its mix of rock superstars and murder. On a balmy Saturday, December 6, 1969, the Rolling Stones were set to play Altamont Speedway in Northern California, and the Oakland chapter of the Hells Angels, led by the charismatic Sonny Barger, had been asked to provide security for the band. It was late in the day and all the opening bands such as Santana; Crosby, Stills, Nash and Young; and Jefferson Airplane had already played and left the stage. As the sun set, the Stones were taking their time, making the massive crowd of over 300,000 fans wait to see them. The crowd got very angry and went crazy when the Stones finally came out, surging into the security barrier in front of the stage. The Hells Angels pushed the crowd back and off the stage, using shortened pool cues as "persuaders."

Then somebody threw a bottle at an Angel, followed by more bottles being thrown. The angry crowd had the audacity to start messing with the Angels' bikes, which were parked in front of the stage area. It doesn't take a genius to tell you that messing with a one percenter's bike is a very bad idea. The Angels entered the crowd, grabbed a few of the vandals, and started beating them down.

A black man in a bright green suit rushed the stage and pulled out a gun. Mick Jagger was singing "Under My Thumb" when Meredith Hunter got up on the stage. He was knocked off the stage before the gun went off. It's generally a bad idea to pull a gun on a one percenter, and it's a genuinely terrible idea to pull a gun on a tense group of Hells Angels. In the melee that ensued, an HA named Allan Passaro stabbed Hunter five times, then the Angels stomped his lifeless carcass into the dirt. They picked up what was left of him and handed the remains over to the medics. When the smoke cleared, an Angel had been shot by Hunter, but that fact is seldom remembered. Hunter died of his wounds and the press had a field day with the riot at Altamont. Even though Passaro was acquitted in the subsequent trial and the killing was ruled self defense, the press portrayed the Hells Angels as monstrous devils and critics called the tragedy the "Death of the Woodstock Nation."

These dudes look like easy riders, living wild and free.

The lesson in *Easy Rider* is that America had sold out, as symbolized by the Captain and Billy themselves (see page 174). Despite the deeper meaning Fonda meant to capture in his film, American youth saw something else: they saw two free spirits having an adventure aboard wild Harley choppers before being gunned down by ignorant southern rednecks. More than one teenager sewed an American flag onto his jacket and went out and bought a bike that summer in search of freedom. Did you?

Fonda came up with the ending of the film first and worked backwards from there when crafting the screenplay with the help of writer Terry Southern. Fonda acted as the film's producer while Hopper directed. At the time *Easy Rider* debuted across the country, the hype about the movie centered around the fact that Fonda and Hopper, along with some of the other stars in the film, had actually smoked real pot in the scenes in which they're seen toking up. In 1969, that was a big deal and people came out to see the movie just to see people get stoned (both on the screen and in the theaters).

Easy Rider was also the first film to use popular rock music effectively within the film. Who can forget the opening credits with the Captain and Billy riding their choppers over the blaring strains of "Born to be Wild"? Peter Fonda once told me that he felt that the Woodstock generation had plenty of passion and its art included notable poetry and music, but that it lacked a movie that stood as its anthem. Fonda gave a whole generation such an anthem with *Easy Rider*.

No biker film before or after *Easy Rider* captures the essence of riding as does this film. To watch those choppers float down southwestern highways in the glory of the golden hour is to know the freedom of piloting a big V-twin. Indeed, in the year following the release of the film, Americans bought motorcycles in record numbers. We all wanted a little bit of that freedom.

Easy Rider spawned a new slew of low-budget biker flicks trying to capture something filmmakers never quite understood in the first place. Like Billy and Captain America, they blew it. But whether they understood the film's allegory or not, movie producers saw dollar signs with the success of the Fonda/Hopper film and if they couldn't capture the magic of the original, at least they'd capture the dollars with their own brand of cycle cinema.

On the small screen, Michael Parks took to the road as a laconic two-wheeled drifter named Jim Bronson on a bright red Sportster in *Then Came Bronson* (1969–1970). In every one of the 26 episodes of this TV series, Parks stops in a small burg in picturesque America to touch a few lives and make

"Hey man, is it true they smoked real pot in Easy Rider?*"*

Back in the early 1970s Easyriders *was a small-time biker magazine. Check out the classy sign and swell T-shirts.*

enough money for some gas and beef jerky before heading down that long, lonesome highway.

Besides timing, both *Easy Rider* and *Then Came Bronson* had in common a romantic view of riding motorcycles. Peter Fonda and Michael Parks both spend a lot of film time pondering their places in the universe, trying to find themselves by taking spiritual quests aboard Harley-Davidsons.

Easy Rider and *Then Came Bronson* caused more than a few teenagers to turn to motorcycles as a way of working out post-pubescent angst. The early 1970s have become known as the flower-power years of sex, drugs, rock 'n' roll, custom choppers, hot rods, disillusioned youth, and rebellion. In 1971, the two-wheeled world was primed and ready for *Easyriders* magazine.

A lot was going on in the motorcycle world at about this time. On a cool, dry day in October 1970, racer Cal Rayborn went to the salt flats of Bonneville near Wendover, Utah, to prove that a single-engine Harley could break the absolute land speed record held previously by twin-engine machines. With a souped-up Sportster engine positioned right behind his head, Rayborn piloted the H-D streamliner down the salt to set a two-way record of 265.492 miles per hour. It was the fastest speed any motorcycle-powered machine had ever attained up to that time.

In 1971 Harley-Davidson turned the motorcycling world upside down by introducing a custom-style motorcycle: the 74-ci FX Super Glide, a cruiser that was the closest thing to a chopper a rider could buy from any dealer. Designer Willie G. Davidson married a Sportster front end to an FL Big Twin frame and designed a fiberglass rear boat-tail fender. The bike was given a Sparkling America paint scheme of red, white, and blue (perhaps as a tip of the hat to *Easy Rider*). The Super Glide marked the beginning of factory custom motorcycles. It is evidence that the Motor Company was watching what custom bike builders were up to and trying to give consumers what they wanted. At the same time the Super Glide hit the streets, two biking friends from Minnesota moved to Southern California and changed two-wheeled history.

Gearheads Mil Blair and Joe Teresi teamed up with magazine editor Lou Kimzey to produce a lifestyle-driven magazine for bikers. Lou had been riding choppers since they were called bobbers and motorcycle clubs had names like the 13 Rebels, Galloping Gooses, and Deuces Wild. Lou had been an editor of drag racing and men's magazines, creating such titles as *Drag Racing*, *Drag Strip*, and *Big Bike*. The two-wheeled trio wanted their new magazine to be completely different from any motorcycle magazine on the planet and succeeded with the irreverent and madcap format that became *Easyriders* magazine.

In the early 1970s, Joe Teresi had already logged over 100,000 on choppers and was known as a custom bike builder in his own right. As well as the technical editor on *Big Bike*, Joe, along with bike builder and parts fabricator Mil Blair, designed many aftermarket parts for people who wanted to build a chopper of their own. Mil was also into cameras and acted as *Easyriders'* first photo editor. Along with these three Paisanos (hence the company's name Paisano Publications), Don Pfeil signed on as editor-at-large and produced editorials capturing the passion of the chopper experience. Other early staff members included copy editor Frank Harding and Louis Bosque, along with an assortment of office cats and dogs.

Motorcycle magazines of that time showcased bikes but not the people who built or rode them. Teresi's idea was to publish a magazine that captured the people behind the custom bikes as well as the wild lifestyle that surrounded them. It would turn out to be the first magazine devoted to the biker lifestyle, a winning combination of custom motorcycles and real bikers.

In June 1971, *Easyriders* magazine was unleashed on an unsuspecting public. Just as Fonda and Hopper's film *Easy Rider* provided a theatrical microcosm of the hippie and biker culture, *Easyriders* focused attention on this crazy and rebellious lifestyle and defined it. The first issue didn't offer a biker chick on the cover, just a wild chop job. Soon, though, the team figured out that sex sells and made sure there was always a pretty girl seen with a custom motorcycle on the cover. *Easyriders* had a definite and tweaked point of view, from the wonky "Takin' It Easy" column of bizarre news stories and weird tidbits, to mind-bending art direction and quirky cartoons. It even invented odd-ball characters like Miraculous Mutha, who was the embodiment of the whore with a heart of gold. The first issue jumped off the shelves and soon the magazine had a life of its own.

Early issues of *Easyriders* featured the tag line, "For the swinging biker" (though this soon changed to "Entertainment for Adult Bikers"), and conjured images of wild parties and fast rides on unimaginably customized machines. The magazine created an image of hard partying bikers and a life where beautiful women were plentiful and begging to go for rides on chopped hogs or between the sheets. The first issues were published bimonthly, and the very first David Mann center spread appeared in the third issue.

David created his first painting depicting the motorcycle culture back in 1963. That painting, *Hollywood Run*, and his customized 1948 Panhead accompanied him to the Kansas City Custom Car Show. There, he met "Tiny," an outlaw motorcycle club member, and a close friendship that would last a lifetime was born.

Tiny sent a photograph of David's painting to Ed "Big Daddy" Roth, a famous car customizer and the publisher of *Chopper* magazine. Ed bought the painting for $85 and David's career as "the Norman Rockwell of motorcycle art" began. He went on to paint 10 more paintings for Roth, who published them in his magazines and offered them as posters.

In 1965, David went to work for Sheffer Studios in Kansas City, where he met Dave Poole, an architectural renderer who taught him how to use the airbrush. Mr. Mann went on to study at the Kansas City Art Institute, further refining his craft.

In 1971, David saw his first issue of *Easyriders* magazine, and an ad for artists, cartoonists, and illustrators caught his eye. The publisher and editor liked his work and he was hired. His center spread art capturing the biker lifestyle illuminated the magazine for over 30 years.

David Mann's art is still loved by bikers everywhere because of his uncanny knack for finding the essence of the lifestyle he loved. His work was derived from personal experiences, and his honesty and authenticity showed in every painting. Many of the wild custom designs seen on the motorcycles in David's paintings actually inspired fabricators to create more extreme choppers. He would exaggerate the rake and stretch of a frame, extend a Springer front end much longer than was popular, or make apehangers and sissy bars reach the sky. Soon, builders began replicating David's designs, making custom bikes that were wilder and wilder.

David always said that his outlook on life was one of having fun, enjoying life and freedom, and not letting the bastards get him down. He passed away on September 11, 2004, but his art lives on and will inspire riders forever.

Artist Hal Robinson also joined the staff early on. His leg-wetting cartoons served to further the image of what *Easyriders* was all about. But the magazine wasn't just about wild times; very early on *Easyriders* established ABATE, which at the time stood for A Brotherhood Against Totalitarian Enactments. Today, the organization stands for A Brotherhood Aimed Toward Education and promotes rider education over governmental legislation. The idea was to create a body that policed governmental policies

Here we see famous Easyriders *biker lifestyle illustrator David Mann trying to procure a new model.*

regarding custom motorcycles and acted as a watchdog for new laws that restrict bikers' rights and freedom. At present, ABATE has chapters all over the country with membership in the tens of thousands.

The magazine was, and still is, a sounding board for readers who kept the biker lifestyle alive through Harley's lean American Machine and Foundry (AMF) years, when the Motor Company was owned by a company most remembered for producing bowling balls. *Easyriders* readers have always been very outspoken, so there has never been any guesswork in finding out what they want. *Easyriders* success over the years can be attributed to the success of the American biker—independent, loyal, and proud. Being fiercely loyal to their Harleys, *Easyriders* readers have given credit when the Motor Company has done something right, but they have been just as vocal when H-D has screwed up.

In the mid-1970s, the Motor Company gave bikers a lot to complain about. When AMF engulfed and devoured Harley-Davidson in 1969, the company was building about 14,000 bikes per year. AMF built a new assembly plant in York, Pennsylvania, allowing Harley to ramp up production. Within a decade Harley was building 50,000 bikes per year, but the rise in production was accompanied by a precipitous fall in quality control. At a time when the Japanese motorcycles were getting better and better each year, Harley was producing some of the least reliable motorcycles in its entire history. *Easyriders* gave disgruntled Harley fans a forum in which to vent their feelings toward the shoddy motorcycles being produced by the Motor Company.

Vowing to always give readers what they wanted, *Easyriders* magazine went monthly with the November 1976 issue. By now the rag had gone from 68 pages to 94 and would soon jump to over 100. Loyal readers had gotten into the act of preserving their biker lifestyle and were sending in artwork, photographs, poems, fiction, true road tales, jokes, and cartoons that exemplified the *Easyriders'* way of life. By 1978, so much good scooter photography was coming in that it prompted the creation of another magazine, *In the Wind*, an all-photography publication. Both publications continued to feature the coolest custom bikes and hottest Harley honeys on the planet.

Easyriders has always been about reflecting the motorcycling world, and as the custom bike scene changed and evolved, so did *Easyriders* magazine. By 1980 the rag was already going through refinements, adding more tech tips and legislative news, offering more color photography, more big bike events, runs, and parties, more gorgeous gals, and wilder art. Cool products produced by bikers for bikers began to appear starting with *Easyriders* T-shirts, belt buckles, boots, and more. This would soon mutate into an entire products division including everything a biker might need, from leathers and riding gear, to tools and bike lifts.

Outlaw bikers and one percenters were given a voice and a podium from which to speak with *Easyriders* magazine. The brotherhood of bikers is strong, a fact the actor/producer responsible for prompting so many of them to take to the road can acknowledge and respect. A few years ago I was with Peter Fonda when a grizzled biker walked up, shook his hand, and said, "You changed my life, man. You are the reason I ride."

Peter stood and talked to the biker for over half an hour. They talked about bikes they had owned, runs that they love to go on, and their favorite places to ride. At the end of their time together, they exchanged hugs like old friends—such is the power of the biker brotherhood.

Afterwards, I told Peter that I thought he was extraordinarily kind to give the biker, a complete stranger, so much time. Peter smiled and said, "Dig man, he has been waiting over 35 years to tell me that. Riding is his life. Of course I gave him my time; that's what it's all about."

Magazines like *Easyriders* and films like *Easy Rider* portray a different view of the one percenter than the one promoted in most mainstream media. They depict a more complex and thoughtful type of motorcyclist than the daughter-raping, village-pillaging Hun the public had grown used to seeing, but the latter two-dimensional stereotype still held sway in the public's imagination throughout the 1970s. Outside the motorcycle world, the average Joe Citizen still misunderstood what bikers were all about. The press continued to blow any slight incident involving motorcyclists out of proportion, reinforcing its simplistic stereotype. To most of America, bikers remained the monsters described in the Lynch Report.

BORN TO SELL OUT

What is *Easy Rider* really all about?

For many of you, the film *Easy Rider* may have changed your life forever. After seeing Peter Fonda astride that stars and stripes chopper, riding across America, you probably had only one wish. More than anything, you wanted to

"I had this nightmare that someday Harley-Davidsons would cost 10 to 20 thousand dollars...."

"...and only doctors and lawyers could afford them. It was a bad trip, man."

"Hey, man, I think I found the rednecks and their truck that blew our brothers away!"

be Peter Fonda or, more the truth, to be Captain America. I hope that there's a little Captain America in each of us. But as much as many of us wanted to believe that the film *Easy Rider* was simply about pot smoking and experiencing the freedom of the road on a thundering V-twin, it is *not* just about two free spirits getting gunned down by those awful rednecks. While Peter Fonda grins his best Cheshire cat grin and stays enigmatic about the mind-blowing movie he created, the answer to what *Easy Rider* is about is right up there on the screen.

"He's not busy being born; he's busy dyin.'"

Most of the world didn't get the message of the film *Easy Rider*. The truth is plain to see if you wade through the allegory. Captain America encapsulates the spirit of what this country was originally based upon. He is hope and the spirit of true freedom from oppression, just as Billy represents the ugly American frontier spirit and the conscienceless masses yearning to consume Mother Earth without compassion. Captain America is Thomas Jefferson's concept of liberty, while Billy is the willingness to burn it all to the ground through mindless consumption.

The term "easy rider" is Southern slang for the old man of a whore. He doesn't have to work, doesn't have to pay for his sex, and gets the easy ride. The film shows us that we have collectively raped and brutalized Liberty and made her our whore. America is still about freedom, but it's the freedom to eat more Whoppers and Big Macs while the rain forests burn. Billy thought that freedom could be bought and sold in the marketplace. You score big and you retired in Florida, mister. Captain America knew that we as a country "blew it" because we stopped being about something and just concentrated on getting that one big score.

Guess what, people. Billy won that argument. Look around you. Just as Captain America and Billy took their cash and bought two-wheeled symbols of decadence and excess, we all ride the highways—a country on luxury wheels and cell phones, a country without roots, without a tribe . . . lost. As such, we're moving too fast to care about our neighbor, to raise a barn, to stop for a downed bro. We're all on the move to get our thing together, score big, and retire in Florida, mister. Yuppiedom is the holy church of personal greed and its members are the "me" generation.

Now, here's the surprise ending: we are racing toward our date with those rednecks in their ancient pickup truck. The sword of Damocles is poised and Liberty is dropping her scale. The lessons are staring us in the face in *Easy Rider*. The bikers stop to fix a flat at a farmer's house. And then later, they stop at a commune. In both cases they meet people who are living off the land and doing their own thing in their own time. They are people who chose to be caregivers to the earth rather than takers and exploiters. The boys ride on toward their doom, refusing to stop, to take a stake and be about something, to join those who are about building something real. Over 37 years ago Peter Fonda made sure Captain America told us plainly, "We blew it." And you know what? All these years later, when our leaders look us straight in the eyes and lie boldly, when a man is measured not by the compassion in his heart for his fellow man and Mother Earth, but by the size of his wallet and toys . . . we're still blowing it, man.

CHAPTER 7

𝖂𝖔𝖗𝖑𝖉𝖜𝖎𝖉𝖊 𝕺𝖚𝖙𝖑𝖆𝖜𝖘

THE SPREAD OF THE AMERICAN BRAND
OF ONE PERCENTER TO EUROPE, AUSTRALIA,
AND BEYOND.

One percenter motorcycle clubs flourished in the 1980s, even with the RICO Act nipping at every outlaw biker's boots like some ravenous wolf. Small clubs of all kinds sprouted up all over the country; some were one percenter clubs, but most were just guys who loved motorcycles and were looking for brothers to ride with.

The media-induced perception that all bikers were the bastard spawn of Attila the Hun was time and time again promoted by everything from local newspapers to national network news. For a long time it seemed that every time some kid stubbed his toe, bikers were blamed for the heinous atrocity. Not that we are an innocent lot. The truth is that bikers are capable of both more and less of the kind of behavior you might expect of us. Bikers are among the most big-hearted and charitable groups in the world, giving to blood drives, boys and girls clubs, children's hospitals, and much more.

Bikers can also be violent. Never corner a wild wolf, my friends, for those teeth and claws are there for a reason. Mostly, violent behavior has been a way for bikers to protect themselves as a group, developed out of necessity back in a time when straight society was more than ready to thump their asses. In the schoolyard, the kid who grows up to be a biker is seldom a bully, but rather the kid who stands up for the little kids and whips the bully's butt. We just plain hate injustice. We also don't care much for authority figures.

So many myths and legends have grown around bikers in the past 40 years, it is nearly impossible to separate fact from fiction. From the rituals surrounding a prospect becoming a patch holder, to the mysteries of church night (when the club's officers meet to do business) and protocol for mandatory bike runs, each club has its own rules and regulations. Some details of being in a one percenter club are universally true. For instance, all the members (patch holders) in a club have a say as to whether or not a hang-around can become a prospect. The prospect in question is usually sponsored into the club by an older member in good standing. That member pretty much stands up for the prospect with the club, in the event the prospect does something stupid (like thinking he is going into the bar with the club instead of staying outside to watch the bikes).

Naturally, the prospect is expected to run his ass off and be an all-around gopher for the club, going for this and going for that. If the patch holders are likened to knights on iron steeds, then prospects are their faithful squires and servants. Sometimes prospects get into clubs quicker by doing a bit of business for the club. This has more to do with proving their undying loyalty to their brothers than to the actual act they have been asked to do. There have been times when prospects have done something to show class to the club and it has backfired and made the club look bad. This is a definite no-no.

For a prospect to become a fully patched member of a club, all the patch holders meet and vote on whether or not he is to be accepted. The day a prospect becomes a patch holder is right up there with the best days of his life—after all, most marriages don't last as long as membership in the brotherhood. One percenter clubs have strict rules on dues, mandatory meetings, runs, and so on. In most clubs you have to have a motorcycle that is up and ready at all times. If your bike is down for more than three months, you might be fined or even tossed out of some clubs. As I said, every club is different and different rules apply.

Some clubs demand that the fully patched member get a club tattoo within a year of becoming a member. To keep the club tattoo hidden from public scrutiny, many get it on their shoulder or back. The patch holder is allowed to have the club logo and motto inked on his body. Such club mottoes include: "God forgives; the Outlaws don't" (the Outlaws MC) or "We are the people that our parents warned us about" (the Bandidos MC).

If one percenters are so bad, why would they bother to stand in line and order politely?

As more and more clubs appeared in America, turf wars began to flare up. If there was more than one motorcycle club in a city, all the members knew where they could safely go and where their safe territory ended. Bigger clubs began taking over smaller clubs (if the smaller club was about something) or snuffing them out. This sort of fighting between clubs has gone on as long as there have been clubs. It is very similar to the wars between different indigenous tribes of people all over the world. Bickering between tribes has gone on in every time and every culture on earth; why should bikers be any different?

Certain major one percenter clubs have long been enemies of one another. Sometimes a slight by one club can cause another club to hold a grudge for years . . . even decades. When you see two different one percenter clubs that have been at war form a truce, it is an uneasy affair. You never know when a beer bottle might break followed by swinging fists, flashing knives, and drawn guns. The feds have had a field day with warring clubs, throwing much unwanted dung into the fire.

In the past decade there have been many books dealing with various informants that the cops have hidden within one percenter clubs, sometimes having the cop inside as a patch holder for years. Let me just say that there is nothing lower in this world than a rat. Regardless of how you might feel about one percenter motorcycle clubs, I have seen good men go down for shit they didn't do far too many times just because they happen to be flying a patch on their backs. Two of the worst problems that one percenter clubs have are police informants on the inside posing as club members, a.k.a. rats, and turncoats, a.k.a. snitches.

Not that turning traitor is anything new. Since the seeds of rebellion were first sewn, man has turned against man if it served him. The fate of Captain William Kidd comes to mind; a man who had a commission from the King of England to hunt pirates became known as one of the world's most famous pirates himself. The testimony of Kidd's mutinous crew of turncoats sent him to the gallows.

As the RICO Act took hold in America and clubs battled against clubs, bikers in much of Europe and beyond began establishing their own American-style motorcycle clubs. Bikers in Australia are known as "bikies." Despite the fact that a bikie sounds like a character on the *Teletubbies*, these one percenters in Australia, as well as in Europe and elsewhere, have become as notorious as their American counterparts.

There are one percenter motorcycle clubs in Canada, England, Ireland, Scotland, France, Belgium, Sweden, Germany, Italy, and Australia, and they are all lovers of custom motorcycles. Some are badass muthas in their own right. In a recent edition of the British newspaper the *Sunday Times*, a report on organized crime in Europe included the following:

> Illegal motorcycle gangs are a global phenomenon with strictly organized chapters located worldwide.
>
> In Europe, three groups are dominant: the Hells Angels, the Bandidos, and the Outlaws. These gangs are involved in crimes ranging from traditional drug smuggling or vehicle crime to human trafficking and contract killings. They are spreading throughout the new member-states but are particularly active in the Nordic countries, in Germany and in Belgium. They are also becoming more active in Britain.
>
> The main gang activity is drug trafficking. Illegal substances enter the European Union (EU) through several principal routes, each dominated by different gangs. For example, routes through the Nordic and Baltic region are dominated by Russian-speaking gangs, while the Atlantic area is in the grip of the Dutch, the British, and the Belgians. These well-established routes have also become corridors for illegal immigration, alcohol and tobacco smuggling, and sex-slave trafficking. Each year, more than 100,000 women and children are trafficked across EU borders. Many end up in forced prostitution in brothels or on the streets of British cities.
>
> Governments and their police forces know they must work together to dismantle such increasingly sophisticated networks.

This supposed worldwide menace had an interesting origin in Europe, where local motorcyclists learned what they knew about one percenter motorcycle clubs from watching American biker movies. Yep, it's true. The great anti-establishment breed of foreign one percenters began with innocent bike lovers watching good old American cinema. Inspired by Jack Nicholson, Bruce Dern, and Adam Rourke, European bikers turned up the collars on their leather jackets and got a little more attitude. After a few pints of Guinness down at the pub, these bikers would burn rubber on chopped Triumphs and Nortons and scare the local sheep all to hell.

In the Wind *editor Kim Peterson in 1979. You can tell he's up to no good.*

Europeans have, in the past, been taken by the very American phenomenon of rock 'n' roll. A British subculture known as Rockers combined music with racing street bikes and more than a dash of teenaged rebellion. While American teens had *The Wild One* and later *The Wild Angels*, the Brits had a film called *The Leather Boys* (1964). Remember that *The Wild One* was banned in England until 1968. *The Leather Boys* director Sidney Furie crafted a black and white gem in this film about working class riders who turned their angst into passion for their precious café bikes.

The 1980s brought a rash of American biker films to Europe thanks to the technological wonder of video tape. For the first time, bikers in Europe could watch films that brought them the exaggerated Hollywood version of the one percenter right in their homes. Imitation being the sincerest form of flattery, many Europeans ran out and started chopping their bikes; some even started one percenter clubs. Since the American biker movies were exaggerated depictions of real clubs, the European clubs started out as wildly exaggerated forms of their American counterparts. For instance, choppers in Sweden are known as being the longest bikes in the world. If a 16-inch over stock Springer front end worked in America, the Swedes would chop their bikes out 30 inches over stock. Disenfranchised youth on both sides of the pond were riding bikes, reading *Easyriders*, watching biker movies, and enjoying the freedom of being in the wind. No doubt about it though, they picked up their cues on biker attitude, slang, and style from America. This meant that a true foreign biker needed a Harley-Davidson to consider himself part of the brotherhood.

At the same time, America was becoming aware of epidemic illegal drug use in its cities and suburbs, and the media was happy to play up the bad news. One percenter bike clubs were easy targets when the public wanted to know who might be supplying America with its pot and coke. A 1982 report from the FBI linked one percenter motorcycle clubs with the manufacture and distribution of drugs. It also cited a link between clubs and prostitution, contract murders, you name it. If it was illegal, one percenters got blamed for it. Convenient, eh? It's a wonder that one percenter clubs weren't blamed for alien abductions, global warming, and Starbucks as well. After all, America is hooked on caffeine, so it makes sense that a biker somewhere is profiting from it, right?

Of course individual bikers engaged in drug trafficking in the 1970s and 1980s; so did just about everyone else, from Joe the postman to college

Brit bikers love their rugby.

students to housewives to doctors, lawyers, and even law enforcement officials. Anyone who came of age in the 1960s and 1970s was either part of the drug culture or a social outcast. That's just the way it was, but that didn't break the media of its addiction to portraying bikers as drug-crazed savages. And having an easy target like motorcycle clubs saved many a lazy policeman from having to bust his balls doing real police work.

Law enforcement officials have long believed that motorcycle clubs are complex criminal organizations. The problem for them is that proving a club's tie to organized crime is extremely difficult and demands major funding for long-term investigations. Sort of a catch 22. The RICO Act was used in the 1970s and 1980s in an effort to shut down the drug trade. Hells Angels Oakland chapter president, Sonny Barger (who has also held the post of the HA's U.S. national president), was arrested on conspiracy and drug charges in 1979. Naturally, the press had a field day with Sonny's arrest; the story made it in *Time* and *Newsweek* magazines with the usual exaggerations. Ever notice that if a one percenter is arrested and they raid his pad and find a hunting knife and a pellet gun, the report mentions confiscating "a large arsenal of weapons?"

This particular case was a media circus lasting eight months. The court demanded that bulletproof glass be installed in the courtroom and that everyone in or out of the building be searched for weapons. Defense attorneys made the point that the RICO Act was unconstitutional since a club could not be held accountable for the actions of every member. When the case was concluded in July 1980, news magazines failed to report that after 17 days the jury could not reach a verdict on 32 of the 44 counts against Sonny, his wife Sharon, and a few others. And the cost to taxpayers after all this wasted time and effort? Oh, something in the neighborhood of $5 million. Your tax dollars at work.

Over time, the RICO Act had decimated most of the one percenter clubs. Many patch holders were in prison, often on trumped up charges; others went into hiding and some clubs collapsed entirely. As Harley-Davidson came out with its Evolution motor in the early 1980s and white-collar workers took to riding new Harleys in droves, many one percenter clubs were changing their image. Motorcycle clubs began getting involved with local charity projects, showing a new face to the public. If they were to survive they had to educate the public and prove that being a member of a motorcycle club did not make you public enemy number one.

Eventually, the media perceived this shift in outlaw attitude and reported on it. In 1990 the *Los Angeles Times* had a headline which read, "Hells Angels Make Good Neighbors in Ventura." The piece had to do with the club's ability to coexist with locals and mentioned its efforts toward raising money for local charities.

Europe and the rest of the world was a decade behind their American counterparts and, as U.S. clubs began to portray a less menacing image, European one percenter clubs took the outlaw stereotype very seriously. Foreign papers reported clubs shooting up and bombing rival clubhouses. There was murder in the streets as clubs fought for turf and took no prisoners.

In 1981 Australian bikies had their own Hollister Riot during the Australian Motorcycle Grand Prix. The animosity between bikers and cops had been brewing for years before erupting at this event, with 90 police injured and 100 arrests made. The cause of this melee? It seems that the police drove over a woman who was sleeping on the ground, effectively scalping her. Their response after the riot ensued? Arrest more bikies.

After another biker versus cops clash in 1985, more than 500 bikers were charged. Sick and tired of the violence, many Australian bikers boycotted the following year's event and attendance plummeted . . . just what the cops wanted all along. In his book *The Brotherhoods: Inside the Outlaw Motorcycle Clubs*, Australian writer Arthur Veno talks about his work in establishing a truce between the cops, the bikers, and rival clubs. He mentions that there is no easy way to get to know a club and that it takes patience and good will on all sides to make a truce work. In 2001, Veno acted as a go-between for cops and the Gypsy Jokers after eight members of the South Australian Gypsy Jokers were arrested in connection with an assault on three special operations officers in a coastal tourist town.

Veno discovered that the club was considered to be a major criminal risk by police, who spent a lot of time and money monitoring it. This included having a police helicopter hovering over the Gypsy Joker's Adelaide clubhouse during its 14th anniversary party. Veno found that the club posed a danger to the community because it had built up a sizable arsenal in order to be ready for inter-club violence. The police thought that the club was amassing weapons to attack local cops. Veno stepped in to successfully defuse the situation.

As a historian of foreign motorcycle clubs, Veno states that he believes the first U.S.-style outlaw motorcycle club was the Auckland, New Zealand, chapter of the Hells Angels, formed in 1961, followed by the Gladiators, a one percenter club formed in 1963. However, it wasn't until the 1970s that outlaw biker clubs hit Down Under and Europe in significant numbers.

Just as the veterans of World War II came home to indulge in the white knuckle thrills found on two wheels, so many Vietnam vets joined one percenter motorcycle clubs when they returned home from the jungles of Indochina. It seems that the dark side of rebellion always flourishes after a war, and Vietnam had more than its share of returning rebels. And the circumstances of that war proved more alienating for returning vets than in any previous conflict. Unlike World War II where returning servicemen were given a warm hero's welcome, Vietnam vets returned to a world that didn't want them. Because of widespread opposition to the war, these vets were often shunned on all sides; they had been let down by the system that had sent them off to fight a political war that lost all meaning. Returning 'Nam vets were rightfully pissed off and ready to have a little fun. For many of them, a chopped motorcycle and a patch went a long way toward making things right.

There are even Vietnam Vet motorcycle clubs but these are not one percenter outlaw clubs. They fall into what some have called 10 percenter clubs, such as many Christian motorcycle clubs. As Veterans Motorcycle Club website states:

> We aren't about territory: never have been, never will be. We are not a one percenter motorcycle club. Nor are we about drugs. We pose no threat to any other club. But be assured that we do take our colors very seriously.

In Europe and much of the world, few outlaw motorcycle clubs actually wear the one percenter patch. This is seen as an elite group, the baddest of the bad, and there has been some controversy among the foreign clubs over who deserves to wear the patch. The Hells Angels in some countries claim that they are the only club who deserves to wear it. However, many outlaw biker clubs in Europe and Australia, including the Gypsy Jokers, Bandidos, Rebels, Odin's Warriors, Descendents, and Coffin Cheaters proudly wear the one percenter patch.

I've mentioned more about Australian clubs in this look at across-the-pond one percenters because Australia has the largest concentration of bikers

Never judge a book by its cover. Bikers raise more money for charities than any other group.

There was a time when bikers sought safety in numbers. A lone rider was constantly hassled by citizens and cops.

outside the United States. There are somewhere between 3,000 and 4,000 outlaw motorcycle club members in Australia, and in recent years much of the inter-club warring has taken place in Western Australia.

Internationally, the four largest outlaw clubs are the Bandidos, Hells Angels, Outlaws, and Pagans. It has been estimated that the Hells Angels alone have somewhere around 10,000 members worldwide, making them by far the one percenter club with the most members. It's no wonder the club is known as the Big Red Machine.

ORIGINS AND EXPANSION OF THREE CLUBS

According to Sonny Barger, former national president of the Hells Angels, a group of bikers were riding around Oakland, California, wearing the death's head patch and calling themselves Hells Angels back in 1957. Then they found out that there were two other clubs in California using the same logo and calling themselves the same thing. One of the clubs was from San Bernardino, the remnants of the Pissed Off Bastards who changed their name to the Hells Angels in 1948, after the Hollister incident. This chapter is generally thought to have been the first chapter of the red and white.

The Hells Angels incorporated in 1966: "Dedicated to the promotion and advancement of motorcycle riding, motorcycle clubs, motorcycle highway safety, and all phases of motorcycling and motorcycle driving." The club trademarked its logo in 1972 and its name in the 1980s. Worldwide, the Hells Angels are said to have over 60 chapters in North America and nearly 40 in other countries.

The Bandidos began in 1966 out of Houston, Texas, as a group of blue-collar motorcycle lovers and has since expanded to become a global one percenter club. Its first chapter in Australia was the Sydney chapter, founded in 1984. Today it has over 250 members in Australia alone. The Bandidos MC claims over 90 chapters in the United States, some 90 chapters in Europe, and 15 chapters in Australia and Southeast Asia.

American chapters exist in Texas, Louisiana, Mississippi, Alabama, Arkansas, New Mexico, Colorado, Nebraska, Nevada, Minnesota, Montana, Oklahoma, Wyoming, South Dakota, Utah, Idaho, Washington, and other states. The club has also expanded into Germany, Denmark, Norway, Sweden, Finland, Belgium, Italy, Luxembourg, France, and the Channel Isles of Great Britain.

In 1935 the McCook Outlaws Motorcycle Club was established out of Matilda's Bar in McCook, Illinois. The club grew to include members from all over the Chicago area, changing its name and logo in 1950. The first Florida chapter was sanctioned in 1967, and in 1977 the first chapter outside the United States was established when the Satan's Choice of Canada became an Outlaws chapter. The first European chapter of the Outlaws MC was born in France in 1993, the Australian Outlaws were formed in 1994, and the independent Belgium chapter joined the American Outlaws Association (AOA) in 1999.

Since 2000, English, Welsh, and Norwegian Outlaw chapters have been added, followed by new chapters in Ireland, Germany, Thailand, and a second chapter in Sweden. The Outlaws MC have continued to expand throughout the United States, Canada, Great Britain, Poland, Norway, Italy, and Russia.

It is clear to see that the very American rebel notion of the one percenter motorcycle club has expanded throughout the world, despite the machinations of the popular media, police harassment, and changing moral values. In today's pasteurized, germ-free conspired consciousness of safety Nazis and industrialized, mindless laborers, the world needs the one percenter now more than ever. In a time when so many go to work every day hating their jobs and feeling disconnected from their lives, we all need to throw a leg over a throbbing motorcycle and raise a little hell. Some of us need to raise more than a little hell, which is why we become bikers.

Much has been written about the violent nature of outlaw bikers. It is true that over the years individuals who happen to be bikers have been found guilty of heinous crimes, including murder. There have also been times when several members of a one percenter club have conspired to commit crimes, including bombing a rival club's clubhouse and even killing members of rival clubs. This sort of crime is more prevalent outside the United States where there is no RICO Act. But as has been proven time and time again in courtrooms across this country, you cannot condemn all the members of an organization because of the actions of a few individuals acting alone.

A word about the concept that one percenter motorcycle clubs are in fact notorious highly motivated masterminds of organized crime . . . sort of a chopper riding mafia. Have you ever met a real one percenter? Ever had a chat with one? If so, you would come away with the firm impression that the man you just conversed with is a lost warrior in a time that doesn't need his services, a Conan without a war in which to wield his mighty broadsword. You would definitely

All a biker needs… assuming there's a woman in that tent.

understand the one percenter's passion for his motorcycle and his club, the two things in his life that he stands for and that stand up for him. Neither his bike nor his club will let him down. They have his back, so to speak.

What you would *not* come away with is the impression you had just met a member of some vast underground empire of doom. And the secretive "church nights", hardly clandestine meetings as holy as some Masonic rite wherein the officers of said club meet in dark stone temples by torchlight to conjure and control a mighty drug empire. No. These guys are lucky to agree on where to go for a bike run or which charity to give the proceeds to. If you don't believe me, check out the rules and regulations of a typical one percenter club—hardly the stuff of Tony Soprano or the Godfather.

CLUB RULES, REGS, AND BYLAWS

Although one percenters are anti-establishment rebels who go their own way, every organization has rules and regulations, and a motorcycle club is no exception. In fact, the bylaws of the average MC are reminiscent of the "articles" that a sailor had to sign before becoming part of the crew on a pirate ship.

What follows is a composite listing of some club rules taken from many different American one percenter clubs. They have been edited in order to be generic and would fit most clubs, but certainly do not cover all the rules of all motorcycle clubs. During church night, the officers of the club hold sway in much the same way as any civic organization such as the Eagles, Jaycees, or Moose Lodge. Robert's rules of order apply. The president of the club along with a vice president, secretary, sergeant-at-arms, and treasurer move the meeting along. Cookies are not served afterwards.

> The rules of the club are strictly enforced. Anyone breaking them will be dealt with by a committee made up of original members. The breaking of club rules could result in dismissal or suspension.

> Failure to pay club dues may result in dismissal.

> All members will wear the club's colors in the prescribed manner with the club logo, club name, and chapter displayed as shown in the club articles.

Prospects will only be allowed to wear the club bottom rocker as well as a prospect patch.

If a group or individual citizen (non-club member) attacks any member, the entire club shall stand behind him and fight if necessary. However, if the member is drunk and aggressive and purposely starts an argument, the rest of the club will remove him or step between him and a potential opponent before trouble starts.

No member will disgrace the club by being a coward. This goes for a prospect as well.

No member will destroy club property purposely.

Members are expected to help out their brothers no matter what.

No member will go against anything the club has voted for and passed.

No members will get together and plan something for themselves on club rides. Their idea will be brought up for the whole club, and the club will participate in anything decided upon.

The club will always stay together on rides, runs, and events and will not fraternize with rival clubs. Members may only leave the group if allowed to by the president or whoever is in charge. All club members will leave together. Anyone staying behind will do so at his own risk and can expect no help (sort of like the pirate's code of "He who falls behind, is left behind").

Members are expected to attend mandatory rides and church night meetings. They must have a good reason for not attending such as work, sickness, bike not running, or jail.

Dues will be $10 per month, payable at every meeting or every second meeting. Failure to pay dues within two weeks of the due date will result in suspension. If dues are not paid within two months, the member will be out of the club. The only exception is when a member is in jail, in which case no dues are expected, or out of town, in which case dues will be expected upon his return.

No female will be a member of the club. Wives and girlfriends will be allowed at certain club runs and parties as decided by the officers of the club. In some cases, wives and girlfriends may be allowed to wear support shirts, "property of" patches and tattoos.

Anyone wishing to become a member of the club must prospect for a period no less than six months and for as long as the officers of the club deem appropriate. When voting a prospect in, the vote of members will be taken as an opinion. The officers of the club have final say as to whether a prospect is voted into the club or not.

Prospects are expected to participate in club affairs, rides, and meetings. They must have a running motorcycle (some clubs insist the bike be of American origin, i.e., a Harley-Davidson) and show a sincere interest in the club and bikes. Prospects will stand behind the club and its members, and will go along with what the majority of the club decides (much like the democracy found on pirate ships).

If the club calls a ride, all members will attend unless excused by an officer of the club. If a member's bike is down, he may pack on another member's bike or ride in the chase truck (usually loaded with girlfriends, tools, and beer).

On weekend rides, members should be able to take time off work to attend. If this is impossible and more than four members cannot attend the run, the club will wait for them the following day.

Church meetings will be closed to all except members, prospects, and those who have business with the club.

Any non-member attending one of our bike runs is expected to follow our rules. If another club attends one of our rides and breaks our riding rules, we will stop and let the club continue by itself.

If a club member is permanently kicked out of the club, his club tattoo must be completely covered or an "X" will be tattooed over it.

Talking during meetings will be kept to a minimum until a member is recognized and given the floor by the president. The sergeant-at-arms will evict anyone who disrupts a meeting.

No one will pass the road captain on a club ride.

The entire membership will vote on where the club will go on club rides.

The treasurer will keep a clear record of all money paid in and out and will report on the balance at club meetings.

All members will attend church meetings on their motorcycles, weather permitting.

A member whose motorcycle is down for an extended period of time may be suspended until his bike is in working order.

No one will lend his colors to anyone who is not a member of the club.

No one will bring heat to the house (meaning that no member will cause trouble or deal in illegal activities that might draw police to the club).

Members will wear their club colors on club rides.

Anyone leaving town for more than six months is expected to leave his colors with the president until his return.

Any member missing a meeting for any reason will be fined $10 unless he is in the hospital, in jail, or out of town for a period of time.

No prospect or member is allowed to use heroin in any form. Hypes will be immediately kicked out of the club.

No explosives will be thrown into campfires for any reason (some clubs state that the fine for such activity is an ass-whipping).

Guns that are carried on runs will not be displayed after 6 p.m.

Club members will not fight each other using weapons. Fights with members are to be one on one; prospects are regarded the same as members.

If a club member fights a member of a different chapter of the club, a fine of $100 will be taken from each man by the treasurer of their club and they may be suspended for a time decided on by officers of the club.

No narcotic burns. When making deals, person gets what they are promised or the deal is off. Breaking this law will get you kicked out of the club.

All fines will be paid to the club treasurer within 30 days. Monies will be held to use for upcoming runs.

If a member is kicked out of the club, he will remain out for one year before being accepted back into the same chapter. Club tattoos will reflect in and out dates when the member quits.

If a member is permanently kicked out of the club, the club tattoo will be completely covered or an "X" will be tattooed through the club tattoo at discretion of the chapter. There are basically two ways to get out of a one percenter motorcycle club. If a member leaves honorably it is most likely that he has served the club well for many years and is still considered a brother though he has retired. The other way is to be "out bad." This means a member has been kicked out of the club for some reason. At best, to be out bad means that he is shunned by the club as an outcast.

CHAPTER 8

The Harley Connection

HOW AN AMERICAN COMPANY FIRST SCORNED AND
THEN EMBRACED THE REBEL WITHIN TO SPREAD THE
BIKER LIFESTYLE TO EVERY CORNER OF THE GLOBE.

A s with the Vikings, pirates, and gunslingers of other times, the biker archetype lends itself to being glorified and mythologized. Bikers are bigger-than-life characters. The perception is that bikers live life to the fullest. If life is a banquet, bikers take big bites.

When average Americans think of an outlaw biker they imagine greasy jeans, engineer boots, a chain wallet, a black leather jacket, long hair, a beard, and tattoos. Every stereotype has a certain amount of truth behind it, and bikers really do dress the part. It may seem odd that a rebellious breed would adopt a standard of dress, but biker attire serves a very practical purpose; most of the things a biker wears are worn for a reason. The leather jacket, gloves, and boots serve as a second skin in case he goes down. Scuffing up a leather jacket is a lot better than sporting road rash all over your back and arms. Likewise, a chain wallet doesn't fly out of your pocket and get lost when you're skidding down the street on your butt. That way you don't lose your beer money.

Plus you'd look like an idiot if you wore non-motorcycling clothes to a biker event. Try showing up at a bike run in shorts and sandals and see if you get any respect from the brothers. At massive motorcycle rallies such as Sturgis and Daytona Bike Week you'll witness a sea of black leather. Imagine all the cows it took to outfit the biker nation. Today's family of bikers includes people of every race and creed, every age and nationality, and every stratum of society: blue collar, white collar, doctors, and lawyers. Put them all in black leather and you have a great equalizer. Suddenly, you don't see a welder or a doctor; you see brothers talking about their machines and the ride.

The biker culture is very specific as to how a biker should look, what he should wear, what music he listens to (Bob Seger, Steppenwolf, and Lynyrd Skynyrd are okay; Milli Vanilli and Tears for Fears are not).

But remember that not all bikers are one percenters, and not all one percenters are members of motorcycle clubs. A one percenter is a biker who lives on the fringe of society. He doesn't fit in with the norm. He is not a 9 to 5 kind of guy. He lives life on his own terms. There are many individuals, such as the biker who posed for photographer Michael Lichter for the cover of this book, who are not members of outlaw motorcycle clubs but are nonetheless one percenters because of their attitude and the way they choose to walk through life.

Hollywood's image of the outlaw biker always has him astride a chromed out chopper, but not all one percenters ride choppers. Many ride customized FXRs for their speed and maneuverability, and many more ride full-dress touring bikes. At a huge biker funeral for one of the Sons of Silence, dozens of the club members rode in formation on touring bikes rather than the choppers you've seen in biker films. Outlaw motorcycle clubs like to travel together in packs and ride fast. A Harley-Davidson dresser will get you across the country fast and in style. One stereotype that proves to be true most of the time is that outlaw motorcycle clubs in America still choose to ride American machines, primarily Harley-Davidsons.

Just as the biker lifestyle has spawned a definite biker look, no one percenter would be without the motorcycle of choice for outlaw bikers everywhere: his Harley-Davidson. This preference began in the early Boozefighter days of the late 1940s, though at the time many riders still preferred Indian Motocycles (correct spelling). When Indian went out of business in 1953, there was only one American motorcycle company left.

The fast, loud bobbers of the 1940s and 1950s, and the sleek, long choppers of the 1960s and 1970s were the ride of choice for one percenter clubs all over the world. The executives at Harley-Davidson weren't thrilled that outlaw motorcyclists were bobbing and chopping its pride-and-joy products and riding them while the company garnered all manner of negative press clippings. But Harleys were the iron steed of outlaws because

Only a Harley-Davidson can match the one percenter's bigger-than-life image.

only Harley-Davidson could match the one percenters' bigger-than-life image. Like their riders, chopped Harleys were perceived as being big, loud, dangerous . . . and very American.

The Motor Company has held an uneasy alliance with the outlaw community. At first, it rejected them outright, but as its marketing savvy developed, it began to see marketable value in capturing the rebel image and making it synonymous with Harley's frontier heritage. Today, Harley-Davidson uses the outlaw image to market its product to riders who want a taste of rebellion, even if only for the weekend. How did this happen?

YOU MEET THE NICEST PEOPLE ON A HONDA

Remember that in the early 1960s the one percent of motorcyclists who were the "bad element" of motorcycling really did comprise one percent or less of the riding community. At the same time, there was only one American motorcycle company left operating. It was during this period when Japanese motorcycles began to hit the market. The Japanese motorcycles were inexpensive, reliable, and easy to use, and the other 99 percent of the motorcycling public began to snap them up in increasing numbers. Honda's snappy advertising slogan, "You meet the nicest people on a Honda," further drew the line between respectable citizens on fast, efficient Japanese bikes and dirty, smelly outlaw bikers on Harleys. By the time AMF put Harley up for sale in 1981, the market for heavyweight motorcycles had declined so precipitously that Harley was losing money and had to lay off 40 percent of its workforce.

Old graybeard bikers will look back and tell you that it was the Harley faithful who kept the Motor Company going during those dark days, that blue-collar bikers on leaking Shovelheads held the faith while H-D reinvented itself. While light, small ci Hondas, Suzukis, Kawasakis, and Yamahas were littering the American landscape, established motorcycle companies such as BSA, Royal Enfield, Norton, and Triumph disappeared.

Harley-Davidson made a huge investment in building and marketing light bikes with its Italian subsidiary Aermacchi, but the effort wasn't enough to compete with the Japanese motorcycle industry. Harley-Davidson advertising for its Italian lightweights made every effort to distance the company from one percenters by showing young American men and women in snazzy sporting attire, ready to play tennis or lounge by the beach, with their Aermacchi Sprints and Toppers looking very straight and stylish in the foreground. The ad copy was equally straight: "Widen your FUN horizons," or "For real fun, ride the real one . . . Harley-Davidson." In fact, the Harley ads looked like clones of ads for lightweight Hondas.

Throughout the 1960s and 1970s H-D kept the one percenter element as distant as possible, even though hardly anyone but one percenters were buying Harleys at the beginning of the 1980s. Then 13 Harley-Davidson executives, including the vice president of styling, Willie G. Davidson, decided to buy out the company from AMF. Part of their motivation involved the loyalty of the outlaw element that the company had been denying even existed throughout the AMF years. Also, Harley had solid business assets and a huge dealer network. However, what motivated the team had more to do with what has been called the "Harley mystique." The Motor Company had become an American institution, and Harley owners all over the world will tell you that there is a very real heart beating inside their Harley-Davidson. This is not something one often hears said of a Honda or Yamaha. Harleys have an intangible quality that goes beyond the motorcycle as a transportation device. It is as if the motorcycle is alive; it is a loyal friend, a comrade in two-wheeled adventure.

The sound of a Harley-Davidson is also unique, so much so that Harley lawyers actually tried to patent the sound of a Harley a few years back. There are those who might argue that the true heartbeat of America is the throbbing "potato, potato, potato" sound of an idling Harley.

As the decade of the 1980s began, it looked as though Harley might follow other famous marques like Triumph and Indian into oblivion. In 1980, rumors of a possible buy-back from AMF were flying around Daytona Bike Week. On February 26, 1981, a group of senior executives from Harley signed a letter of intent with AMF to purchase H-D. The purchasing group was led by Vaughn Beals, an AMF executive in charge of Harley operations, and included the company president Charles Thompson, William G. Davidson, and others in the company. The 13 Harley executives who bought Harley-Davidson back knew that they had the most loyal customer base in the history of American products. A Harley enthusiast was more loyal than Chevy or Ford owners or Coke or Pepsi drinkers. Harley had a stronger customer base than Levi's or Budweiser or Crest. In short, no other motorcycle was a Harley and the 13 execs knew it; that was the strength of the company and why they agreed to go to extraordinary lengths to keep their very American company going.

Harleys weren't the only bikes that were turned into choppers. That's a Honda 750 Four on the left and a Triumph on the right.

The Harley mystique is a value that is hard to explain to those who do not ride. The experience of owning and riding this great motorcycle is as uniquely American as rock 'n' roll. No other American company has a following that is so loyal that they have that company's logo tattooed into their skin for life. That's dedication.

Proud Americans rallied to Harley-Davidson as the Motor Company improved its product and re-invented itself as a maker of dependable, quality machines. The Harley Owners Group (HOG) was established in 1983 to offer Harley buyers a factory-sponsored motorcycle club. HOG held a wide range of activities, from rallies and events put on by local dealerships to national parties. Within six years there were over 90,000 HOG members worldwide.

I remember talking to Clyde Fessler, a Harley executive who had a lot to do with HOG and the reinvention of H-D's marketing after the buy-back. "The Japanese were kicking our butts," Clyde recalls. "We had to ask ourselves what we could do that the Japanese could never do. The one thing they could not touch was that [we were] American. We used that. That is when we created the Harley logo of the eagle holding the Bar and Shield." Harley's great strength was that it was the last American motorcycle company. At the time, Americans were sick and tired of hearing about how well the Japanese were doing; they were selling more cars, more TVs and electronics, more motorcycles. There was a growing sentiment in this country to "buy American," and Harley used that eagerness for American products to its advantage.

The marketing division of Harley-Davidson used the American flag and the eagle to great effect in reminding Americans who they were and where H-D stood as a company. While it had tried to latch onto the squeaky clean image that Honda was known for, Harley eventually saw that the rebel spirit was a big part of its legacy and embraced it, even using skulls, flames, and other outlaw images on bolt-on hard parts and in its clothing line.

Americans are tenacious and Harley-Davidson has become known as a company that is a survivor. The average potential Harley rider likes that fact. Since its humble beginnings in 1903, H-D has survived many major crises that threatened to put the Motor Company out of business. For instance, Harley's motorcycle production soared from just 150 units in 1907 to 28,000 in 1920. When consumers switched to automobiles for primary transportation, its motorcycle production plummeted by 10,000 units a year. The Great

Bikers wear Harley gear with all-American pride.

Depression also took its toll on H-D; production dropped to just 3,700 bikes by 1933. While the need for military motorcycles for World War II helped production, sales nose-dived after the war. Harley was ill-equipped to handle the Japanese motorcycle invasion of the 1960s and 1970s, as its products were thought of as inferior. Harley production skyrocketed in the AMF years, but high production caused low quality control and consumer confidence plummeted. Harleys were thought of as outmoded, oil leaking dinosaurs. The reality matched the perception; a saying at the time was: "Harleys don't leak oil, they mark their territory."

The one thing that the Japanese could not do was be an American motorcycle company. Harley realized that it should do what it does best, namely build big, heavyweight motorcycles. Its failed experiment from 1968 to 1978 of marketing an assortment of lightweight and middleweight bikes proved that dealers and customers wanted a Harley to be a Harley—a big American motorcycle. The dealers wanted the higher profit margins that big bikes afford and H-D realized that the American people did not associate the Motor Company with small bikes.

As the 1980s rolled around, it was time for Harley to reinvent its image a bit. It still built bikes that were perceived to be outmoded, and it had not had a new motor configuration since 1966. In 1973 Harley owned 77.5 percent of the 851-cc and above motorcycle market. By 1980 Harley's numbers had dwindled to just 30.8 percent. It was time to do something.

After long and bloody negotiations with lenders, the 13 executives of Harley-Davidson mounted up for a truly historic ride. On June 16, 1981, a large pack of Harley riders, led by Willie G. Davidson, took off from the York, Pennsylvania, facility. Harley dealers and riders joined the pack as they rode to a Pittsburg dealership and spray painted over the AMF logo on the Harley-Davidson sign. The word spread all over the world: "The Eagle Soars Alone." Even in this time of triumph, the Japanese motorcycle companies continued to gain ground. By the end of 1981 Harley lost its coveted hold on the heavyweight motorcycle market to Honda. For the first time in its history, Harley was no longer the king of the heavyweights. The Motor Company was running low on funds and quality was still an issue.

On September 1, 1982, Harley's chairman Vaughn Beals filed a petition with the International Trade Commission for tariff relief because the Japanese were dumping their bikes into the U.S. market with big discounts and in huge numbers. On April 1, 1982, President Ronald Reagan signed a temporary heavy tariff on Japanese motorcycles over 700 cc to give H-D some breathing room.

At the same time, Harley was developing its Porsche-designed Evolution motor. When Harley introduced the 1,340-cc V2 Evolution engine in 1984, it opened up an entirely new market for its products. Having the ability to overhaul your own bike was no longer a prerequisite for Harley ownership. Now anyone with the coin to buy one of the big, expensive American machines could join the Harley fraternity.

The Porsche-designed Evolution V-twin motor was seven years in development. It produced more power and was lighter, cooler running, and extremely oil-tight when compared to its Shovelhead predecessor. The new FXST Softail, which captured the hardtail look while retaining a functioning rear suspension by hiding gas shocks beneath the frame, gave the American biker a motorcycle hewn from the stuff of chopper legends. The company began offering demo rides at its dealers, and in no time at all, upscale baby boomers who had always had a soft spot in their hearts for Harleys and had enough disposable income bought the new machines in record numbers.

Willie G. and his team were creating a new breed of motorcycle to wrap around the new engine, machines aimed at the Harley faithful. They wanted to bring them bikes that featured the latest technology while looking like nostalgic Harley classics such as the Hydra Glide. In 1983 Harley formed HOG and held regional rides and rallies for HOG members. In many ways HOG was Harley's way of creating its own motorcycle club, as it had seen the close ties that being part of a club provided for riders. HOG quickly grew to over 100,000 members. Some say that the creation of HOG was the smartest move that the management team came up with to ensure customer loyalty. Plus HOG acts as a two-way communication tool; it keeps Harley management in touch with the wants and needs of its customers and also gives the customers a direct link to the latest news on the Motor Company's new models, rides, events, and so on.

New H-D advertising campaigns pushed the fact that new Harleys no longer leaked oil. One famous ad shows a group of grizzled bikers glaring at the camera. The ads says, "Would you sell an unreliable motorcycle to these guys?" Harley was clearly making fun of its bad boy image and using it to the company's benefit for the first time. The old adage, "If you can't beat 'em, join 'em," seemed to be working big time. Reliable bikes plus the ability to provide factory customs allowed H-D to attract a whole new customer.

While one percenters may have originated many of the custom chopper styles, Willie G. went to rides and rallies all over the country and was always looking for styles and trends to use in new Harley models (see p. 222).

The FXST Harley Softail of 1984 looked a lot like a bona fide chopper with its fat bob gas tank, long wide glide front end, pullback handlebars, and forward mounted foot pegs. The seat was of the king and queen variety so popular with choppers of the 1970s, and the hidden shock swingarm design made the frame look like a rigid, or hardtail, just like the choppers of old. Plus the Evolution (Evo) motor was a bulletproof design that refused to leak any oil on garage floors. Over the years, whenever Harley came out with a new motor or added a new innovation, such as electric starters in 1965, the Harley faithful were slow to embrace the new technology. But with the new-fangled Evo motor and the new Softails, many riders wanted the new machines as soon as they became available; Harley had a hit on its hands. It also had another hit when it took the wraps off a new model motorcycle known as the Fat Boy in 1990. This stripped FL-styled Softail is still one of the factory's most popular models.

This had a tremendous impact on the demographics of Harley's customer base. Within a few years Harley's median customer evolved from a hard-riding, hard-partying one percenter, to a fellow (or gal) who tended to be a bit older, better educated, and have a higher income level than other motorcycle owners.

As the Evo era progressed, Harley continued to court a more affluent customer base, both in the motorcycle market and in the stock market. In the summer of 1987 Harley-Davidsons roared down the streets of Manhattan to announce that Harley-Davidson was listed on the New York Stock Exchange. A Harley Heritage Softail was proudly displayed above the floor of the Exchange and the Harley flag flew outside. Harley's executives motored down Wall Street escorted by New York's Finest, also on Harleys. In the years since, Harley-Davidson has continued to be a very American success story, one that mirrors the fierce independent nature of the one percenter. Both are rebellious free spirits in a world of conformity.

Harley had turned itself around and, by the end of 1987, enjoyed an $18.7 million stock offering. Harley's share of the 851-cc and up motorcycle market went from 23.3 percent in 1983 to 46.5 percent in 1988, while Honda sales in the same market dropped from 44.3 percent to 24.1. Harley continued to sell every motorcycle it could make, and sales were up to $757.4 million in 1988.

Harley-Davidson had clearly realized that part of the American dream was the dream of outlaw bikers, that nonconformity has its place in the motorcycle culture. Moreover, Harley accepted that Harley riders live their dreams and explore their fantasies. Bikers aren't afraid to twist their throttles on an open stretch of road. The Harley faithful of old-school bikers had not only kept the torch from going out, but they had also fanned the fires of rebellion and lit the way for a whole new generation of riders. These were men and women who were also trying to find a way to live their dreams and would find them aboard Harley-Davidson motorcycles.

In 1990 motorcycling lost one of its greatest ambassadors. Billionaire publisher and avid motorcycle rider Malcolm Forbes traveled the world aboard Harley-Davidsons, presenting a very American image of independence, freedom, and good will. Harley offered up a tribute with the biggest motorcycle parade in history at that year's Daytona Bike Week. In his introduction to the 1990 book, *Well Made in America*, Forbes sums up his passion for Harleys, and his words hit home for many of us who ride:

> For heart-and-soul bikers, their dream's reality is saddling up their machines, whether it's to go down the block for a beer and a look or to reach the farthest corners of the country and sometimes the globe.
>
> For many of us and perhaps most, Harley-Davidson seems to embody that spirit of freedom more than other machines. A good part of the feeling, of course, stems from the fact that Harleys are the only U.S.-made motorcycles in an industry overwhelmingly dominated by Japanese models.
>
> But there's far more to it than that. For instance, there's the intense satisfaction of knowing from the action, the feeling, and the sound when you've shifted gears, that the husky Harley engine sounds could never be confused with those of a sewing machine or a lawnmower. Harley saddles fit better. Your own seat lasts longer, tires less after hours on 'em.
>
> Today's durably handsome Harley visibly embodies the colorful past in its powerful present. The Harley mystique is a reality to its rider. If Harley had gone belly up, as it damn near did a few short years ago, a real part of our heritage, an American tradition, would have gone with it.

In a way, bikers symbolize the American spirit; they are rebellious and strong, and they don't take any shit.

In 1990 *Easyriders* magazine had a banner year. With over 200 issues under its belt and bringing readers the best of the biker culture for 20 years, the magazine was ready to do something big, something unprecedented. On July 14th, with the sponsorship of American bikers everywhere, *Easyriders* went to the salt flats of Bonneville with its twin Harley Shovelhead-powered streamliner and took the absolute land speed record away from Kawasaki. The 322.150 mile per hour world record held for 16 years.

In August of that year Sturgis, South Dakota, held its 50th Annual Rally and Races. Over 300,000 bikers rode in from all points on the globe to be a part of the event that the late J. C. "Pappy" Hoel and the Jackpine Gypsies started in 1936. Naturally, *Easyriders* was there and pulled out all the stops to celebrate its 20th anniversary with all of its readers, as did the Motor Company. Special for 1991 was a bike that recalled the look of the Shovelhead Sturgis edition. The FXDB Dyna Glide Sturgis was a blacked-out factory custom featuring a totally new frame and rubber-mounted motor. Hot on the heels of this scorchin' hoop-de-doo, Daytona had its 50th anniversary of Bike Week and Laconia had its 70th birthday. As always, if you made it to these mega-bike events, you might've just found yourself in *Easyriders'* glorious pages.

By the end of 1991 Harley-Davidson had earned a whopping 62.3 percent of the market share in the 850-cc and larger motorcycle category, and had the imported bike companies on the run. Just as with the Sturgis 50th, Harley came out with a limited edition 1992 Daytona Dyna Glide with special paint and graphics to commemorate 50 years of the ultimate run to the sun. The Motor Company celebrated its 90th birthday in 1993 with specially trimmed models, and began offering fuel-injection on certain models in 1995. Annual production had reached 100,000 units and dealers still couldn't meet public demand. With so many riders plunkin' cash down for American-made motorcycles, the climate was ripe for bike-buildin' entrepreneurs to step in and make a buck.

The midway mark of the 1990s decade acted as the starting flag for a number of new motorcycle companies. The Indian motorcycle was trying to make a return, as was Excelsior-Henderson. There was talk of a new Vincent, and Triumph was making a surprising resurgence. At the same time, several small companies with names like American IronHorse, Titan, California Motorcycle Company, Big Dog, and Ultra were rattling their bike-building sabers using S&S motors and aftermarket transmissions, along with the best products from American companies producing complete custom factory motorcycles.

Of these new companies, Polaris with its Victory motorcycle seemed to be the most promising and well funded. As the Excelsior-Henderson ad banners said in 1998 at Sturgis, "This ain't a one horse town anymore." Seemingly overnight, more and more S&S powered custom bikes started popping up. The courts took the Indian name away from Eller Industries and awarded it to Indian/CMC. Suddenly it looked as though the "Big Three" of Harley-Davidson, Indian, and Excelsior-Henderson might rise from the ashes like some motorized phoenix to create a second Golden Era of motorcycling.

Not that Harley was daunted by these young upstarts. The Motor Company held a huge party in Milwaukee in May 1998 celebrating 95 years of motorized excellence. Ninety-fifth anniversary models all featured special paint and trim, and the Road King was the most popular bike in America. For 1999 Harley slapped the aftermarket with its completely new Twin Cam 88-ci motor and a slack-jawed world of riders could only look on in awe. This revolutionary 1,450-cc powerhouse would rocket Harley into the new millennium in style. Year 2000 models even included completely new Twin Cam Softails with the Twin Cam B motor, guaranteed to be as smooth as glass on an emerald pond.

Harley's success and its ever-improving model lineup made its motorcycles increasingly accessible to average riders, completely changing the image of Harley-Davidson riders in the public's eye. As the new millennium got underway, the only people who still saw Harley riders as murderous berserkers were those who had spent the previous quarter century marooned on some island that lacked a satellite television antenna.

But where did this changing demographic leave the original one percenters? Certainly leather clad bikers had gone mainstream, and upscale, white-collar workers on Harleys filled up the parking lots of drive-in restaurants across the country on bike night. But what of the real one percenters?

In 1994, no less an icon of the one percenter lifestyle than Sonny Barger was interviewed by the *Los Angeles Times*. He was profiled as an entrepreneur, selling his own line of salsa and even T-shirts that proclaimed, "Sonny Barger—American hero." While many would say that Sonny had mellowed with age, the famous Hells Angel still proclaimed, "I just believe we have a right to do anything we want to do as long as we're not hurting anyone else, and if anyone tries to stop us, we have a right to step on them."

Many smaller one percenter motorcycle clubs around the country had been swallowed up by bigger clubs. Others downsized or disappeared due to RICO Act harassment. By the 1990s the original wild ones were getting older, many becoming grandfathers. Into this ever-changing motorized landscape a new rider was emerging. Known as the rich urban biker, or rubbie, this new breed of weekend warrior would both aid and annoy the one percenter world.

HARLEY'S FACTORY CUSTOMS

Harley-Davidson production models that took design elements from the one percenters' custom choppers.

When it comes to the look and feel of a Harley-Davidson, one man's name leaps instantly to mind: Willie G. Davidson. Most of the Harley faithful agree that Willie G.'s design changes may have saved Harley-Davidson from extinction. As the grandson of Arthur Davidson, Willie was born into motorcycling. At motorcycle runs and rallies, Willie G. is Harley's best spokesperson and is an almost mythic character in the biker community. There is no one in motorcycling who is more revered and loved.

How did Willie G. become the heart and soul of the Harley look? He graduated from the Art Center College of Design in Pasadena, California, and went to work for Ford Automotive designing futuristic cars. He then did general industrial design for Brooks Stevens Design Associates in Milwaukee. In 1963, his father, William H. Davidson, then president of Harley-Davidson, gave Willie a call. William H. wanted H-D to have its own in-house styling department and wanted to put his son in charge of it. Willie G. told his father, "Give me five minutes to pack my crayons and I'll be right over."

Growing up with Harleys around him, Willie is a true biker and the first Harley executive to sport long hair and a beard. He knows what Harley riders want because he is truly one of us. I can't tell you how many times I have seen him at Sturgis or Daytona during their bike weeks, crawling around on all fours, looking at every detail of a motorcycle. He lives for this stuff and his love of motorcycles shows in everything he does.

Willie G. has single-handedly been the keeper of Harley heritage, designing bikes that bikers love. He watches the trends and keeps his fingertips on the pulse of the two-wheeled world. In 1971 he created the first factory custom:

By the mid-1980s, stock Harleys were looking more and more like custom choppers.

The FXS Low Rider used many of the styling cues found on custom bikes.

the Super Glide. Willie did what bike customers were doing; he took a stock FLH Electra Glide and stripped it of its windshield and saddlebags, then gave the bike a custom rear fender and seat. He married a Sportster front end and skinny front wheel with the creation, creating the Super Glide, a factory machine that captured the custom look of a chopper.

The Super Glide was the first in a long line of custom creations by Willie G. Davidson. What follows is a list of some of the bikes that changed the way the world viewed Harley-Davidson. These were motorcycles that the riding public had to have. They encased the spirit of H-D in designs that utilized the latest technology, yet kept the raw Harley look and feel that bikers wanted and demanded.

1971 - FX 1200

Willie G. married an FL frame with a Sportster front end and came up with the Super Glide, the first factory custom. Its red, white, and blue "Sparkling America" paint scheme may have been a tip of the hat to the popular film, *Easy Rider.*

1977 - FXS LOW RIDER

The FXS looked every bit like a custom bike, with its mag wheels, lettered tires, and drag-style handlebars. The bike offered custom paint and special engine treatments, taking the factory custom look to a new level.

1980 - FXB STURGIS

Harley gave up on the light and middleweight Aermacchi bikes in 1979 and introduced several new bikes in 1980. The 80-ci, blacked-out Sturgis model was bad to the bone and offered a belt primary and final drive.

1980 - FXWG WIDE GLIDE

The 80-inch Wide Glide was everything a one percenter could want. With its wide Electra Glide front end (sans chrome shroud), apehangers, custom flame paint job, and king/queen seat with sissy bar, the bike looked like a real custom chopper.

1983 - XR-1000

This badass little sportbike was a handful of fun with its XR-styled racing heads by Jerry Branch. Not a chopper, but one percenters love performance and this scoot was like a Sportster on steroids.

1984 – FXST SOFTAIL

The first factory custom to sport the new 1,340-cc Evolution motor, the Softail looked even more like a chopper than the Wide Glide. The trick was the Softail frame with its hidden gas shocks, which created a hard-tail look.

1984 – FXRDG

Harley's light and fast FXR in a Custom package with two-tone paint, wrinkle Evo engine, and lots of chrome, included a chrome solid-disk rear wheel, which lent the bike its Disk Glide (DG) designation. The limited-edition FXRDG was offered in this year only.

1986 – FXST-C SOFTAIL CUSTOM

The Softail was a hit and Harley began offering it with a five-speed instead of a four-speed transmission. The Custom version included a solid rear wheel, upgraded two-tone paint, a better seat, and engine trim that included a wrinkle black finish and lots of chrome.

1986 – FLST HERITAGE SOFTAIL
AND FLST-C HERITAGE CUSTOM

Harley figured that if the chopper look worked, so would the nostalgic Hydra Glide look . . . and H-D was right. These bikes utilized FL-style front ends and fenders on Softail frames.

1987 – FLST-C HERITAGE SPECIAL

The "C" designation stands for "custom," and this version of the popular Heritage Softail included soft leather saddlebags, windshield, and a two-piece seat with backrest.

1988 – FXST-S SPRINGER SOFTAIL

Basically, this was the FXST Softail with Harley's newly redesigned Springer front end incorporating gas shocks for a smoother ride. This bike was reminiscent of the cool Springer choppers from films such as *Wild Angels*, but with all new technology.

1990 - FLST-F FAT BOY

If an FXST looks like a chopper, this stripped down FL looks like a bob-ber with a fighter-plane paint job. The Fat Boy was very popular and included solid disc wheels front and back, dual exhaust, and a special styling package.

CHAPTER 9

The Rebel in All of Us

THE BIRTH OF THE RUBBIE (RICH URBAN BIKER): LAWYERS IN LEATHERS, DOCTORS ON WHEELS.

Imagine a time before laptop computers and cell phones, a time when most men worked with their hands to earn a living for their families. It was not all that long ago. In 1984 Harley-Davidson was producing the last of its Shovelhead motors and the first of its Evolution motors. The oil-leaking, ride-it-and-repair-it world of blue-collar American motorcycles was coming to an end. Up until the advent of the Evo motor, you had to have a tool kit strapped to your bike if you intended to ride it. Then the Evo-powered Harleys appeared on the scene and almost overnight the two-wheeled world changed.

Traditional bikers looked at the Evo motor with disdain. As previously mentioned, the Harley faithful were never ones to accept change easily. A popular T-shirt summed it up best: "See no Evo, hear no Evo, ride no Evo." But as the Reagan era wound down, many Americans had something called disposable income, which could be used to purchase things they wanted to have but didn't strictly *have* to have. A $16,000 motorcycle is *not* as essential as a roof over your head, but essential or not, a whole lot of upscale Americans went out in droves to buy new Harley-Davidsons.

Willie G. Davidson's nostalgic Softail bikes reminded baby boomers of the motorcycles with which they grew up. When you look at a Heritage Softail, something inside you says, "Now that's a Harley." The Softail line was not only a brilliant marketing move, but it was also an efficient, reliable product. The bikes were oil tight and the Evo motor led to the first stock

Harley that you could ride for 100,000 miles without an engine overhaul. Remember that before the Evo, riders were used to having to tear their motor down every 20,000 miles for a rebuild.

At *Easyriders*, roving reporter Rip Rose took a first-year Softail across the country nearly every month to report on biker happenings and to hang out with brothers from coast to coast. He couldn't believe that the Evo motor just kept going and going, like some sort of two-wheeled Toyota. After logging 100,000 miles on the bike, Rip took the heads off and looked inside. The aluminum motor looked as clean as the day it rolled out of the factory. He just buttoned her back up and kept on riding. The Softail was still in Rip's stable and a loyal everyday ride until he passed away a few years ago.

The reliability of the Evo-powered Harley-Davidsons of the mid-1980s created an entirely new generation of Harley riders. For the first time, you didn't need to have a lot of knowledge about engines to ride a Harley. Hell, anyone could do it. I remember walking into Bartels' Harley-Davidson in Culver City back in 1984 and drooling all over a new Softail Custom. An old-school biker was glaring at the machine and said to me, "You know what's wrong with these new Harleys?"

"What's that?"

"They'll sell 'em to any rich asshole who wants one."

Riding a motorcycle in America had become a brotherhood. If you rode a Harley, you were instantly a brother of the road. If you broke down by the side of the road, other bikers would stop and help you get your bike going again. If the bike needed more care than a roadside fix, they'd take you home, put you up for the night, and get you and your scoot to the nearest reputable dealership the next day. They took care of their own because no one else would ever dare to stop and help "one of those damned long-haired scooter tramps." That's why Harley riders still wave to each other as they pass. It's an unspoken camaraderie . . . we're brothers.

The Evo motor changed all that. I ran my hand over the leather seat of that Softail Custom in Bartels' and up walked salesman Gene Thomason. Gene's a lifelong biker and knows where all the bodies are buried. He smiled and said, "You know what they say, there are two kinds of people in this world: the ones who own a Harley and those who wish they did." Gene was right. Baby boomers came out of the woodwork to buy the new, modern Harleys. Some were empty nesters. They had owned motorcycles in high school or college, then had gotten rid of them when they had families to raise "because the

Unlike the reliable Evolution-powered Harleys introduced in 1984, riders of ironhead Sportsters didn't leave home without a complete set of tools.

wife says them murdercycles is too damned dangerous." Once the kids were out of the house, these guys started looking at the Harleys with affection. They'd bring their wives into dealerships and sit them on the passenger seats.

Back then, many Harley dealerships would let you take the bike around the block if you were a really serious potential buyer. That cinched it. Empty-nest couples found a new way to connect with each other on the roads of America aboard powerful, gleaming Harley-Davidsons.

Gene sold me that Softail Custom by the way. I traded in a leaky Shovelhead for it.

The new bikes drew a lot of business professionals who had never been on a motorcycle before. These white-collar guys saw a new Harley as a status symbol. After all, most blue-collar Shovelhead riders couldn't afford to just plunk down $16,000 for a new Evo bike. But doctors, dentists, accountants, lawyers, and stockbrokers found a new form of freedom aboard their new Softails. These professional men had high stress jobs, trophy wives, and big mortgages to pay. For a few hours every weekend they could don brand new Harley leathers, start up their Harleys with the touch of a button (you didn't have to spend a half hour sweating over a kick starter), and roar off, disturbing their uptight, upper income neighbors. They'd spend a few weekend hours catching a little wind and feeling the freedom that riding brings.

Riding a Harley became a lot safer with the advent of the new Harleys, too. The new Evo-powered Harleys were bulletproof, and new riders could take a run down to the corner bar or cross the country without worrying about breaking down in some redneck town to await the fate of Captain America and Billy. And as an ever-increasing portion of the other 99 percent of riders took to the roads on new Harleys, there were fewer and fewer bigoted rednecks trying to gun them down. In fact, a good number of the motorcycle haters depicted in the film were now riding Harleys themselves.

The fact that upscale riders were entering the market en masse created a whole new industry to support their wants and needs. Harley-Davidson's HOG catered to the new riders, offering local rides and fellowship for men and women to get together and enjoy their passion for Harleys. When you buy a new Harley, you are instantly enrolled in this club, which also provides better deals on bike insurance, a touring service much like AAA, maps, emergency road service, a listing of all the dealerships in the country, and even a fly and ride program. When you buy a Harley, you buy into a gigantic family, a community dedicated to having a good time wherever they ride.

At the same time, Harley got less affluent new riders to enter the fold by offering a hell of a deal on new entry-level Harley Sportsters. You could buy a new Sportster for $3,995, sell it back to Harley within two years, and apply the full $3,995 toward a Big Twin Evo Softail, FXR, or dresser model. This encouraged many women to throw their legs over their own Harleys as riders instead of passengers. Today, women riders comprise up to 35 percent of new Harley owners in many states. While women have never been allowed to be members of one percenter motorcycle clubs, there are many mainstream motorcycle clubs for them.

The coming of the rubbies created a wider gap between the haves and the have-nots. Part of the biker lifestyle includes the concept that anyone who is bold and brash enough to ride a Harley deserves some small modicum of respect. When rich urban bikers showed up at major bike runs, such as the Sturgis Rally in South Dakota or Daytona Bike Week in Florida, more often than not, they trailered their bikes to the rallies. They would stay just outside of town, pull their bikes off the trailers and then ride the last few miles into the event with their new leathers gleaming in the sun.

This sort of activity pissed off the one percenters. After all, riding is about riding, right? Rubbies were seen as having no heart, no guts, as being worthless, rich sissies. There was even a popular biker T-shirt that proclaimed, "I rode my bike to Trailer Week!"

Still, the blue-collar and white-collar riders mixed together at bike events and rubbed elbows, though the rubbies generally washed their hands with disinfectant soap after shaking hands with any real one percenter. While bikers who had been in the lifestyle most of their lives seethed over the newbies and their *Cigar Aficionado* world of jet setting, big business bullshit, there was a positive side.

Once you become a Harley rider you take up the bar and shield as part of your heart and soul. The new rubbies joined motorcycle rights organizations such as ABATE and began to use their big bucks and connections to defeat mandatory helmet laws in states across the country. When legislators would meet to discuss helmet bills, they were used to ragtag groups of blue-collar bikers showing up to protest. This changed when the rubbies came to town with their celebrity friends. Lawmakers suddenly had to face off against riding lawyers and such pro-motorcycle notables as Jay Leno, Peter Fonda, and Larry Hagman.

Another positive effect of rubbie riders was that they poured big bucks into anything and everything associated with motorcycles. Suddenly, local

The annual California Redwood Run is still one of the best old-fashioned, roll-around-in-the-mud biker parties imaginable.

bike shops, many of which were run by old-school bikers, were filled with work, turning stock Harleys into custom bikes. The motorcycle aftermarket began to swell with new products to feed the rubbie horde. These mild ones spent money on their two-wheeled passion—big money. It was nothing for a rubbie to buy a Harley for $16,000 and then spend another $16,000 on chrome, parts, accessories, and custom paint.

Every year, Harley-Davidson production increased to meet the new demand for bikes. Pushed by new riders in an explosion of motorcycle consuming, Harley was producing over 200,000 bikes per year by 2003. There were just not enough bikes to supply rubbie demand. If you wanted, say, a new red FXSTC Softail Custom from the late 1980s throughout the 1990s, you had to put your name on a list along with a deposit and wait three to six months for your bike to arrive at your local dealership. Naturally, new motorcycle companies began appearing, offering bikes that already looked customized to fill this demand. These pre-fab choppers allowed a new rider to look bad-to-the-bone without ever having to turn a wrench. This also pissed off the one percenters, who believed that bikers didn't deserve to ride if they couldn't wrench on their own bike. But the fact that many traditional bikers owned these new aftermarket companies meant that they were forever in bed with the new riders, for better or worse.

With the creation of this enormous industry, custom bike builders ramped up and began to make a lot of money. This was something new. Back in the 1970s and 1980s, the country's top chopper builders were barely getting by. The market for choppers was just not that big, and many of the people who rode choppers were outlaw bikers. Bike shops, such as Denver's Choppers, were known for building everything you needed to create an awesome long bike, plus they'd build it for you if you wanted them to. On the East Coast, Dave Perewitz and, in the Midwest, Donnie Smith fed the loyal with gorgeous custom bikes. On the West Coast, Arlen Ness and Ron Simms produced high-end customs. The glut of rubbie money turned these venerable builders into superstars.

Custom builders who have been around for a few decades all know each other and even hang out together at bike runs and events. They get to hang with people of like mind, whom they respect, and trade customizing stories, tall tales, and the like. Curiously, this led to the ultimate anti–one percenter club. What's the complete opposite of a one percenter motorcycle club? The Hamsters.

This fraternity of motorcycle mavericks today comprises the elite of industry insiders. Within their membership of several hundred, you'll find owners of aftermarket motor companies, frame manufacturers, custom wheel makers, seat designers, custom bike fabricators, and custom painters. The Hamsters are the crème de la crème of the custom universe. This club began, innocently enough, when several custom bike builders got together to party and ride together during Daytona Bike Week in 1978.

Custom painter and bike builder Dave Perewitz remembers that he and his wife Susan were staying with some friends and bike builders at the Mystic Sea Hotel right on the beach. "One of my best and oldest friends, Jimmy Leahy, decided to dive off of the third-floor balcony of the hotel into the swimming pool," Dave recalls. "He dove into three feet of water with no problem and we all cheered. Well, nobody would ever believe Jimmy did this, so we had to get some photographic evidence. Naturally, we had to have him do the stunt a few more times to get it on film. Jimmy dove into the pool from the third-floor balcony three times, and, boy, was the manager lady pissed!" Miraculously, Jimmy managed to do this without paralyzing or killing himself, but the miracle didn't impress the manager. Dave had to talk her out of throwing Jimmy out of the place.

"Back then, there wasn't the amount of people going to bike week as you have now days," Dave says. "We used to ride our bikes all day, go out to the Cabbage Patch [bar], go see the drag races, go back to the room to freshen up then go out to dinner."

One of the legends regarding the formation of the Hamsters was that it was designed to be the opposite of a one percenter bike club. In fact, one Hamster once jokingly told me that the club has an ordinance in its bylaws that states you can be fined if you block an exit just in case a fight breaks out.

"We started the Hamsters as a joke," Dave Perewitz laughs. "We had these paper plates that we taped to the doors of our hotel rooms in Daytona that said, 'Hamsters.'" Bike Builder Donnie Smith had artist Dave Bell draw up a cartoon of a smiling hamster riding a chopper and had some T-shirts made up. The shirts were bright yellow, as the perfect statement that the Hamsters would run from any fight and were, therefore, "yellow."

"We first wore those shirts when we all stayed in Spearfish, South Dakota, during the Sturgis Motorcycle Rally in 1978," Dave smiles. "The rest is history." And history it truly is. The Hamsters include such world-class custom bike builders, riders, and notables as Arlen Ness, Dave Perewitz, Donnie Smith,

Grady Pfeiffer, Paul Yaffe, Arlin Fatland, Rick Fairless, and Fred Kodlin.

Like the Hamsters, there are hundreds of mainstream clubs that cater to every avenue of the motorcycle culture. There are Christian motorcycle clubs, veterans' clubs, police and firefighter clubs, clubs for BMW, Yamaha, Triumph, Honda riders, etc. If you have an angle, there's a bike club for it. Yes, there are even gay and lesbian bike clubs, like Dykes on Bikes.

Once people began to take notice of the now-familiar yellow T-shirts at motorcycle rallies and runs around the country, the Hamsters soon became an icon for high-end custom bike builders and riders. What is the opposite of the Hamsters? No, not the Hells Angels, rather, the opposite of the upscale, champagne dream world of these Rolex riders is the Weasels.

The Weasels also began as a joke. In 1993, several editors and writers from *Easyriders* magazine were having a few beers at a local watering hole in Agoura Hills, California. The topic of conversation was the importance of just riding motorcycles, rather than being involved in all the chic leathers, new billet aluminum parts, and $5,000 Easter egg–colored custom paint jobs that adorned so many custom bikes at the time. The group was weary of hearing about supposed bikers who trailered their bikes to a bike event and then rode for a few minutes to show off while talking on their cell phones, probably to their stockbrokers. If the Hamsters epitomized the new, upscale biker image, the Weasels was just a bunch of motorized misfits who could give a shit about new parts and fancy paint. Its motto, "A legend in motorcycling since earlier this week," became the standard of this group of comedians on wheels.

To explain the Weasels' place in the riding cosmos, original member Kai Raecke wrote a tongue-in-cheek article, as quoted in the sidebar of this chapter, which appeared in *Easyriders* magazine.

THE WEASELS
A Society of Temporarily Useless, Pissed Idiots and Drunks (S.T.U.P.I.D.)

PART I
INTRO

As of this writing, which is being written today, it being December 1st, 1996, also known as the first day of the twelfth month in the year of our lord nineteen-ninety-six, Weasels have proliferated throughout the land so

Unfortunately, most one percenter clubs have become choked with rules. Riding should be about freedom and fun, not rules and regulations.

profusely that they have become more of a pest than the wholesome entity they originally were intended to convey. Although The Weasels were originally founded with the idea that rules are for morons, too many morons have become Weasels, necessitating rules and bylaws and, in effect, negating the entire purpose of The Weasels.

Be this as it may, I, Red Baron (aka Kai Raecke, Intergalactic Associate Editor of *Easyriders* Magazine), have bestowed upon myself the heavy task of creating these rules and bylaws, after having conferred with a majority of Founding Weasels (or at least one, which ever may have come first), henceforth known as The Grand Weasels. Therefore I, Red Baron, being of half ways sound body and mind and not too drunk at this time, hereby decree the following rules and bylaws in the name of The Original Weasels (henceforth known as The Really Grand Weasels), with the majority vote of at least one other Grand Weasel implied and enacted.

But first, something important:

PART II
A HISTORY – BRIEF VERSION

There have been Weasels.

And now, something even more important:

PART III
A HISTORY – THE LONG VERSION

The Society of the Weasels (S.T.U.P.I.D.) was founded, if memory serves, around the 30th of February 1993. The Original Weasels (henceforth known as The Damn Grand Weasels) consisted of nine or ten or twelve or so frustrated and drunken editors a-editing, scribes a-scribing and other associates a-associating for and with *Easyriders* Magazine and its sister publications (such as *Biker,* and *In the Wind*). These Original Weasels are henceforth known as The Grand Fucking Weasels.

Sitting at Casa Rea, the Original Watering Hole of The Original Grand Fucking Weasels, this above-mentioned group came up with what they thought was an antidote to an admittedly and thusly perceived uppity and snobbish club called The Hamsters. The Weasels, by their very nature, have no money, ride shitty bikes, drink cheap beer, and only wanna have fun that doesn't cost a lot of money. One might say, in general terms, it was a direct outgrowth of the dismal pay conditions the Original Weasels (henceforth known as The Really Grand Fucking Weasels) experienced at the hands of their employer, as well as the constant confrontation with super-expensive bikes with lots of bolt-on accessories and high-tech goodies belonging to lesser rodents, the ability of others to produce aesthetically and technically pleasing bikes, the inability of The Original Weasels (henceforth and for the last time known as The Motherfucking Grand Weasels) to do likewise, and the specific jealousy stemming from these self-evident reasons.

Since their inception, The Grand Weasels have spawned numerous outgrowths worldwide and have multiplied so prolifically that now these newer Weasels, or Follower Weasels (aka Follo-Weas) have looked up to the Grand Weasels imploringly and asked, nay begged, for guidance in the form of rules and bylaws. After long deliberation, much libation, against our better judgment, it being no better than none, and after repeatedly coming to the conclusion that rules are for morons and bylaws not much better than in-laws, we the Grand Weasels have decreed the following section of Rules And Bylaws.

And now the really important part:

PART IV
RULES

1. There are no rules . . .

2. . . . except those rules that are written on these pages.

3. If other rules are deemed necessary for the future existence of The Weasels as a whole, refer to Rule No.1.

4. If Rule No. 1. does not apply, refer to Rule No. 2 or No. 4, unless Rule No. 3 suffices, in which case all other Rules are null and void.

5. There is no Rule No. 5.

And now the really, really important part:

PART V
BYLAWS

A) General

1. There are only thirteen or so Grand Weasels (see Part III, History—the long version, above). They are life-long members of The Weasels without

This Sportster's nickname fits it perfectly.

Riding lets you clear out the cobwebs. There's nothing like being out on the road with just your bike and a good brother.

possibility of parole. They may denounce their membership in front of others, but they are still Grand Weasels, until death or wife do them part, both being the best antidotes to fun known to man.

2. All other Weasels are Follower Weasels (henceforth known as Follo-Weas) and can lose their Weasel birthright and membership at any time and for any reason not deemed worthy a Weasel by either a majority vote of Grand Weasels or a junta of lesser Weasels, after securing their authority from a majority of the Grand Weasels, if possible, but not exclusively.

3. As a member of The Weasels, you are a figment of your own imagination.

B) Specific

1. Being a Weasel is not an honor bestowed upon anyone.

2. Being a Weasel guarantees you nothing but an orange T-shirt, which still needs to be paid for.

3. Being a Weasel implies no recognition among other clubs or organizations as such. The Weasels are a loosely structured, haphazardly thrown together conglomeration of societal misfits and pranksters who like to party and get shit-faced. This is the only purpose of The Weasels.

4. Being a Weasel means never having to say you're sorry.

And now, something you all have been waiting for:

PART VI
MEMBERSHIP RULES

As this is a chapter of Weaseldom which seems to cause the most problems and consternation, we have decided to dedicate a whole Part (Part VI, this one) to it.

Subpart A:

Entering Weaseldom

Anyone may become a Weasel, as long as he is deemed worthy of the cause by at least five other Follo-Weas or two Grand Weasels, unless he is such a worthy human being that no Weasel or even Grand Weasel could surpass his worthiness, in which case he is too worthy to be a Weasel and thus not acceptable as a member.

Subpart B:

Ejection from Weaseldom

Anyone (with the exception of the Grand Weasels) may be ejected from the Glorious Empire of the Weasels if:

a) The Grand Weasels say so (singly or in unison).

b) A junta of at least three Follo-Weas decide upon it.

c) The Weasel in question shows up at a Weasel gathering on a Jap bike.

d) The Weasel in question behaves highly un-Weasel-like (see bylaw c, Subpart A, Part VI of the Weasel Bylaws, e.g.)

e) One or two Follo-Weas want to get rid of someone, in which case he or they need the vote of at least another Follo-Wee or the counsel and authorization of the Grand Weasels (singly or in unison).

And now something extremely important:

PART VII
WEASELETTES

Subpart A:

Weaselettes, or the female version/lay/object of desire/etc. of a Weasel is always a welcome sight, and there are never enough Weaselettes. Although the Original Weaselettes, the Grand Dames of Weaseldom, have long since passed into history and their names have become part of Weasel lore, no one remembers their names; only their faces and bodies still linger in our memories. A single rule pertains to the subject Weaselettes: If they're able-bodied and willing, let's have them.

Subpart B:

Weaselettes, as described above, are to be treated as equal members of our society (S.T.U.P.I.D.). Therefore, they have no rights and may lay no claim to such. They may lay, however, any Weasel they like, as described in Part V, Subpart B, bylaw No. 4. A Weaselette's only purpose is to provide pleasant surroundings at any Weasel gathering and comfort the wounded and dying.

But wait, there's more:

PART VIII
NEW CHAPTERS

Unlike most intelligent books, this little volume is written in parts only and therefore has no chapters.

And for your added illumination:

PART IX
AUTHORIZATION AND ENACTMENT
OF WEASEL-RULES AND BYLAWS

This authorization and enactment of The Weasels Rules and Bylaws is made valid by the signature of a majority of Grand Weasels (or the ones available at the time), attached below. These are the Ten Commandments of Weaseldom and are to be obeyed as such. Any infraction of above described and outlined rules and bylaws will be punished severely and may result in the exclusion from the Glorious Empire of Weaseldom.

And now, for the Grand Finale:

PART X
COPYRIGHT AND PATENT RULES

The Weasels is an official society (S.T.U.P.I.D.) and as such implies all legal and illegal ramifications. The Weasels© is a registered trademark and may not be copied, published or otherwise proliferated without the consent of The Grand Weasels.

Patent pending.

Signed:
The Grand Weasels

In the decades that followed the introduction of the Evo, the rubbie culture has grown to include many hundreds of thousands of motorcyclists all over the world. Harley-Davidson has expanded likewise and its licensed products and collectibles now include every possible gee-gaw, from Harley-Davidson gourmet coffee and Christmas decorations, to sandals and slippers, toys and miniatures, blue jeans and socks, watches and clocks, you

Sometimes you fall off the bike. But this young lady looks damned good, cast and all. She'll have a great story to tell her grandkids.

An early Digger-style bike, popular around San Francisco. The frame is stretched out long like a dragster, but the front end is stock.

name it . . . even motorcycles. While the rebellious motorcycle culture grew wings to include every sort of person, many rubbies today turn out to be high-end businessmen in their 50s and businesswomen in their 40s seeking a way to lower their stress levels and enjoy a little of the freedom promised to them by this country. As Dave Perewitz told me, "These businesspeople who ride turn out to be just like the rest of us; they love motorcycles and love riding."

While the old time blue-collar bikers and one percenters may resent today's rubbies, they will all certainly agree that rubbie money paved the way for an incredibly diverse motorcycle aftermarket. The rubs fueled such companies as American IronHorse, Big Dog, Big Bear Choppers, and other manufacturers of quality factory custom bikes. Many of these motorcycles have price tags that begin in the low $30,000 range. High-end builders such as Paul Yaffe, Arlen Ness, Jim Nasi, and Matt Hotch have built bikes that cost over $150,000 apiece for celebrities, sports figures, businessmen, and corporations.

I recently paid a visit to my friend Rick Fairless at his bike shop and biker bar, Strokers Dallas. I asked him what was paying the bills these days. He pointed out two old-school bikers with long hair and beards who were strolling through the showroom. "See those guys?" he twanged in his rich Texas accent. "Those are our people. It's where we all came from, blue-collar Shovelhead riders. I'll be lucky if they buy a set of spark plugs from me." Then he pointed to three businessmen in suits and ties on their lunch break who were looking at a $35,000 Big Dog motorcycle. "See those guys? Two of 'em bought new bikes from me last week and now they're bringing a friend in to get a bike. That's what's paying the bills."

Certain activities engaged in by both old-school bikers and rubbies alike have helped change the general public's opinion of motorcyclists. In the past 20 years, bikers have become known for their philanthropic tendencies. Clubs and independent riders, rubbies and one percenters alike, have devoted more time and money to charities in this country than almost any other organized group. These charities range from helping the victims of the 9-11 tragedy, to aiding the families of our servicemen and women in Iraq, and raising many millions of dollars to help defeat such diseases as muscular dystrophy, breast cancer, diabetes, heart disease—the list goes on and on.

The one thing that all bikers, whether rubbie or one percenter, agree on is their love for children. Biker groups of all kinds pitch in each year to help the Boys and Girls Clubs of America, the Ronald McDonald House, Juvenile Diabetes Research Foundation, Muscular Dystrophy Association (MDA), and to raise money for the support and care of children with life-threatening diseases through children's hospitals around the country.

One of *Easyriders'* sister publications, *V-Twin*, aimed at mainstream riders of all brands of motorcycles, has taken up the torch for several charities that it sponsors annually. For over 10 years the *V-Twin* Biker's Ball has raised millions of dollars for the Boys and Girls Clubs of Broward County through upscale rides and auctions. *V-Twin* has also joined with the Seattle Children's Hospital, raising millions through their children's ride, charity auction, and gala. The money raised pays unsupported care costs for children with life-threatening or terminal diseases. Bikers of every kind and creed have joined together each year to give back and to do something good in the world, and because of these charity rides and events, the media has begun to see a new side to the leather-clad horde. Local news crews began showing up to watch bikers riding to children's missions on their Toys for Tots runs, and along the way, bikers stopped being the bad guys and became seen as knights on iron steeds.

While there are literally hundreds of motorcycle groups and organizations currently producing charity rides and events across the country, the following is just a taste of a few of the more popular ones: Bikers 4 Kids; Bikers Against Drunk Drivers (BADD); Bikers Against Child Abuse (BACA); Mickey Jones' Foundation for Children; Kyle Petty Charity Ride Across America; the Love Ride (which alone brings in over a million dollars a year); Pony Express Relay for Breast Cancer; Rebels with a Cause; Rip's Bikers Against Diabetes (BAD) Ride; Seattle Children's Ride, Auction, and Gala; and the V-Twin Biker's Ball.

If you are reading these words, get involved with a motorcycle group near you and do some good in the world. There's nothing better than riding your motorcycle for a good cause. To find out more about these and other biker charities, visit www.travelingbikers.com. A good friend of mine once said, "Anyone can make a living; the real challenge is to make a difference."

Whenever a trend reaches mass proportions, it is usually picked up on by the media. Much of the fear and paranoia regarding one percenter bikers and clubs has come from media manipulation, but in recent decades the media has helped create the stereotype of the kinder, gentler biker. Movies and television have aided in selling the idea that motorcycles equal freedom.

Honda motorcycles even have a model of bike called a Rebel. Want to be a rebel? Now you can buy one.

There's no doubt that the film *Easy Rider* inspired a lot of teenaged males to go out and buy a motorcycle. Recent films like *Wild Hogs*, which plays with all the clichés of riding motorcycles, from getting bugs in your teeth to standing up for what you believe in, have also generated interest in motorcycles.

While *Easy Rider* painted a portrait of the biker as mythopoetic hippie, *Wild Hogs* takes the rich urban biker and one percenter alike to task. The plot involves four rubbie riders who decide to take a motorcycle adventure from their homes in Columbus, Ohio, to the Pacific coast in California. The film stars Tim Allen, John Travolta, Martin Lawrence, and William H. Macy as four middle-age buddies who cope with their mid-life crises by donning leather jackets and taking off on their motorcycles for a cross-country road trip.

Through a series of events brought about by the group's clinical inepti-tude—the sort of slapstick bungling that drives the plot of many low-brow comedies—the heroes of the film run afoul of a bike club comprising the sort of stereotypical, two-dimensional one percenter characters that populated the biker exploitation films of the 1960s and 1970s. This anachronistic club is led by a genuinely psychotic Ray Liotta, who becomes more than a little irate when the main characters accidentally blow up the club's bar. Hilarity ensues, or so hoped the producers, mostly in vain, though the film does have its moments along with a cameo from *Easy Rider* star Peter Fonda.

Despite the fact that this 99-minute movie is pure fluff, there are messages to be had about being who you really are, about loyalty and brotherhood and stereotypes. *Wild Hogs* might be the anthem for the rubbie generation of riders who are trying to find a little peace and freedom in a world that makes little sense.

A more interesting aspect of the film is how it portrays one percenters. The depiction is every bit as inaccurate and incomplete as the portrayals in the classic biker flicks of yore, but with the added element of humor. Even Ray Liotta's sociopathic character is treated in a comic manner. In 2007, that old boogeyman monster known as the outlaw biker is now irreverently poked fun at in movies rather than feared. This in part reflects the relative rarity of the true one percenters, who are comprising an ever decreasing portion of the riding public (0.01 percenters?). The leather clad menace on a roaring Harley who pulls up next to your station wagon or mini-van is more likely your accountant, lawyer, or dentist out for a weekend putt than a genuine one percenter. Many of the one percenters who remain among us have earned a certain degree of respect from the general public. As the old wolves of war get long in the tooth, they garner praise from the strangest places.

Even Sonny Barger has become a media darling, publishing his tales of the bad ol' days. There are currently rumors of a movie deal based on his best-selling book, *Hell's Angels: The Life and Times of Sonny Barger and the Hell's Angels Motorcycle Club* (2001, William Morrow and Company). Sonny followed up the success of his first book with a second, *Ridin' High and Livin' Free* (2002, William Morrow and Company). These days Sonny enjoys the same celebrity, notoriety, and mythic status as such legendary rebels and rogues as Captain Kidd, Blackbeard, Billy the Kid, Jesse James, and Buffalo Bill. Watching Sonny shake hands, sign his books, and take pictures with adoring fans makes me think of what it might be like if people today met Cochise, Crazy Horse, or Geronimo. It isn't every day that you meet a real warrior and Sonny is the real deal.

Sonny's popularity these days mirrors the change in the media's perception of bikers. Thanks in part to the rubbies and the fact that bikers raise so much money for charities around the world, the police harass bikers less and the public embraces us more. This is not always a good thing. It used to be that no one would ever dare to touch or sit on a biker's Harley. They might get the crap beat out of them, right? Nowadays, with the advent of so much friendly biker TV assaulting the airwaves, people think that all bikers are friendly. I had one brother walk out of a Denny's to find a whole family of tourists taking pictures of their kids on his Harley. He set them straight . . . fast! Don't ever touch a biker's Harley.

As the world entered the twenty-first century, Harley-Davidson had become stronger than ever before. In 2003 every Harley owner worth his or her salt mounted up and rode to Milwaukee to see where his or her baby was born. The city pulled out all the stops to celebrate the 100th anniversary of Harley-Davidson. Over 250,000 bikers showed up to party with the company that spawned a lifestyle.

It has been a long, strange trip from World War II veterans getting a little crazy with beer and bikes, to the outlaw bike club as criminal syndicate, to the homogenized idea of the biker as just another middle-aged rich American having a mid-life crisis on a hog. Believe it or not, things were

Rebels with a cause raise millions of dollars each year to help kids in need.

about to get even stranger, as the mass media turned its relentless gaze on a new subject for prime time sport. Modern day bikers and custom bike builders were about to get the 15 minutes of fame that Andy Warhol had promised us all.

CHAPTER 10

Marketing the Rebel

A LOOK AT THE PHENOMENON OF MASS MARKETING
THE AMERICAN REBEL: JESSE JAMES, BILLY LANE,
THE BIKER BUILD-OFF TV SERIES, AND THE
ACCEPTANCE OF THE BIKER CULTURE IN
MAINSTREAM SOCIETY.

There have been relatively few television series focusing on the motorcycle rebel over the years. For a short time in 1969, NBC's *Then Came Bronson* filled the bill, and many thousands of new bikers were born after watching laconic drifter Jim Bronson (Michael Parks) ride his Harley Sportster through picturesque America. In the 1990s a syndicated series called *Renegade* followed Reno Raines (Lorenzo Lamas) as a renegade cop turned bounty hunter astride a Harley Softail. Reno was on the run from the law after being framed for murder. Although the two TV series were worlds apart in concept, they both focused on the freedom found on the open road on two wheels, only with Michael Parks, there was a lot of guitar playing, and with Lorenzo Lamas, there was a lot of shooting of shotguns. Believe it or not, Americans can be a pretty gullible lot and many ran out in a frenzy to buy motorcycles after seeing TV shows like these, eager to experience the wind-in-the-hair stress management system known as riding a motorcycle.

Then, not long ago, something happened that changed the motorcycle aftermarket in a major way, for both better and worse—something called reality TV. This obsession with voyeurism focused on watching people of all kinds, from Ozzy Osbourne and his family, to Playboy bunnies shaving their legs.

At the turn of the twenty-first century there was a short-lived TV series called *On the Inside*, which took in-depth looks at odd occupations. The show featured a rodeo clown and an underwater welder and was looking for a custom bike builder for its next episode. TV Producer Hugh King called me up (Hugh had worked as a video editor for *Easyriders* several years before) and asked me to help him find just the right bike builder for the program. This builder had to be young, off the hook, and had to work in Southern California. As the editor of *Easyriders*, I'm in contact with most of the quality custom bike builders around the country, so I am a good source of information on the motorcycle industry in general. I was more than happy to help Hugh out.

In early 2002, I took Hugh to meet Jesse James at West Coast Choppers in Long Beach. I pointed out the shark tank, the pit bulls, the spider web fencing, and Jesse with all his angst and edginess. Hugh knew instantly that Jesse would be good TV and the *On the Inside* show became *Motorcycle Mania*, which aired on the Discovery Channel. The episode brought in the highest ratings ever for a cable network show. Naturally, *Motorcycle Mania II* and *III* followed, as did the *Monster Garage* TV series. Metal maverick Jesse James became a household name in the great tradition of his namesake outlaw of the Old West. Supposedly, Jesse the bike builder is distantly related to the original James family of Wild West gangsters.

Jesse got his 15 minutes of fame and then some. After several seasons of *Monster Garage* (a show about transforming cars into lawn mowers, boats, hot dog machines, flamethrowers, and the like), Jesse married the talented and beautiful movie star Sandra Bullock and is living happily ever after. But what Jesse did with *Motorcycle Mania I, II* and *III* ignited the whole country. For the first time, young people got the message that they didn't have to work in a cubicle when they grew up. Jesse's mantra was that blue-collar jobs were respectable, even artistic. He would smash flat metal with a hammer, coax it into the shape of a gas tank, and then lay down welds so perfectly that they could be on a display in a modern art museum. Suddenly, working with your hands was cool, being a bike builder was ultra cool, and riding a custom chopper was the coolest thing of all.

Motorcycle sales were on an upward climb, factory custom choppers were selling like hot cakes, and the Discovery Channel had a hit on its hands. It took the powers that be at Discovery a while to figure this out. Executive in Charge Jane Root, newly arrived to the Discovery Channel offices in

Maryland from her home in England, disliked the trend of Discovery moving away from science and exploration in favor of what she called "testosterone TV." While Ms. Root was not interested in seeing any more television in which the hosts have tattoos, the public clearly was in love with seeing how motorcycles were made.

At about this time, Pilgrim Films and Television Inc. out of New York shot a pilot with a relatively new custom bike shop in Rock Tavern, New York, called Orange County Choppers (OCC). The owner of the shop, Paul Teutul Senior, was a lifelong biker and ironworker who made his living creating ornamental iron fencing. His son, Paul Junior, was skilled in metalworking and wanted to build custom bikes. OCC was the shop created by father and son, and before they had a TV show, they showed up in Daytona Beach, Florida, for Bike Week. The Pauls had created a lavish, weird, long bike themed after Spiderman. Paul Jr. even rode around Florida wearing a way too tight Spiderman costume to draw attention to the bike and their company. Some of the legitimate bike builders at Daytona just thought the OCC bike was goofy as hell. Then the impossible happened.

The pilot for a TV show called *American Chopper* featuring the crew at OCC went before the bigwigs at the Discovery Channel. Most of the show was about building a bike and that part was fairly boring. But there was one scene where Paul Sr. came out of his office and yelled at Paul Jr. to "hurry up and get off his ass and get the freakin' bike done!" or words to that effect. The Discovery suits in series development raised eyebrows and evil smiles shone on their pallid pates. "We want more of *that*," they hissed . . . and a hit television series was born, whether Jane Root liked it or not.

The Teutuls' hour-long shows revolve around building highly customized "theme" bikes against the clock. These bikes run the gamut from looking like a fire engine, to the space shuttle. As the series went into season two and then season three, four, and so on, the producers milked every possible theme for a custom bike imaginable, even making one that looked like a reindeer for the holidays. The series became known to Americans as "that show where the dad yells at his kid." The custom bike building definitely took a backseat to the mockumentary drama of the Teutuls fighting. Although these badmouthing battles were not scripted word for word, they were created by the directors, producers, and Teutuls in much the same way that TV wrestling is done. The result was that people tuned in to see if this would be the week Senior would smack the tar out of Junior.

Rolling one for the road. Bet he never thought bikers would become TV celebrities.

Once again, America loved the idea of blue-collar workers making good and enjoyed watching the Teutuls' rise to stardom. As their bike business picked up, we soon saw the family trading in their rusty cars and driving expensive Hummers and Prowlers. We saw Paul Sr.'s new mansion. Life was apparently good for the Teutuls. The message of *American Chopper* is less about bike building and more about how anyone can make it big in America. A nice plot device for most episodes includes the fact that the Teutuls often build bikes for charities and raise money for good causes. The boys from Rock Tavern became American heroes and ratings soared. They even appeared in TV commercials for America Online during the Super Bowl halftime show. Jane Root must have been seething.

Soon, the *American Chopper* merchandise machine kicked in, offering eager fans everything from OCC T-shirts and caps, to sunglasses, toy bikes, books, sheets, lunch boxes, CD-ROM games, even cologne. While OCC was flying high, many venerable custom bike builders were appalled. One very famous upscale builder told me that the Teutuls' show destroyed what legitimate custom bike fabricators had spent a lifetime building. Specifically, custom builders had been fighting the traditional biker image for over 30 years. Just when they felt they had been able to gain some modicum of respectability and dignity, and were taken seriously as artists, *American Chopper* showed up to prove that the best way to put a bike together was with a hammer and a lot of yelling. The thought of some builders was that *American Chopper* made custom builders look like the classic stereotype of the dim-witted, knuckle-dragging, bad boy biker—a stereotype they had worked hard to extinguish.

I recall having a conversation with Paul Sr. about fame, fortune, and the bike industry. He told me that he knew they were very lucky and had come along at the right place and the right time. He also knew that the TV circus would end as quickly and amazingly as it began. In short, he was riding the good fortune pony until the wheels fell off. It's important to remember that the Teutuls are playing parts in their show. Despite his on-camera persona, Paul Teutul Sr. is a clever businessman, a good father, and a compassionate and caring man. He'll probably smack me for saying that.

Once the TV business suits at the Discovery Channel realized that Americans had a true love affair with custom motorcycles, yet another TV series appeared on the scene. Hugh King, who had produced *Motorcycle Mania I, II*, and *III*, as well as many episodes of *Monster Garage*, went on to

"Hey, aren't you Jesse James or Indian Larry or something?" "Sure baby, I'll be whoever you want."

produce the popular *Biker Build-Off* series. It should be noted that Hugh works for Thom Beers of Original Productions. Hugh is now the co-executive producer with Beers on the *Biker Build-Off* series, which has moved from Discovery to the Learning Channel (TLC), along with *American Chopper*.

As fate or luck would have it, whenever Hugh needed expert master bike builders to design and build a custom motorcycle against the clock (TV just *loves* when things happen against the clock), he would call me and ask, "Who's hot? Who's next?" So for good or ill, you have me to thank or blame for bringing such diverse and wondrous builders as Billy Lane, Paul Yaffe, Dave Perewitz, Indian Larry, Mitch Bergeron, Chica, Jerry Covington, Mondo Porras, Kendall Johnson, the Detroit Brothers, and others to the small screen. Sorry guys, I know the TV sword is double-edged at times and fame has its price.

This TV series was originally called *The Great Biker Build-Off* and every episode pitted two very different bike builders against each other in a race against the clock to build a custom bike in 30 days and then ride it to a motorcycle event somewhere. Once at the event, a people's choice vote would be called for the best of the two bikes and the winner would advance to another episode. After the first few episodes of this limited run series, the Discovery Channel saw the ratings soar and ordered more episodes. The build time was reduced from 30 days to just 10 days in order to pump up the stress and get builders to throw hammers and yell at each other. Sound familiar?

The first episode of the *Build-Off* pitted Florida rowdy rebel builder Billy Lane against upscale Arizona builder Roger Bourget. Billy and Roger rode their new custom scoots from Florida to a motorcycle event in North Carolina called the Smoke-Out and Billy won the popular vote. For episode two, "Indian" Larry Desmedt from Brooklyn was chosen to go up against Paul Yaffe, a builder that is truly his opposite.

Paul Yaffe creates sleek and original works of motorized art from his shop, Paul Yaffe Originals in Phoenix, Arizona. While Paul is known for covering his chassis with swoopy bodywork and lavish paint schemes, Indian Larry liked to see every nut and bolt on his sparse creations. If Larry's bikes remind one of the insides of a pocket watch, Paul's customs are more like a slick Ferrari. So, in this teaming up of Paul against Larry, you had old school against new thought, North against South, East against West, old veteran against young gun. Hugh King often put two builders against each other that had little in common in order to cash in on the drama and to see how people would vote.

For Indian Larry's entry in this particular *Build-Off,* he created a tribute to his mentor, Ed "Big Daddy" Roth. The *Rat Fink* bike (as it became known) was the perfect Indian Larry machine. Larry liked to see all the parts of the motorcycles exposed. He liked to see all the gizmos, the clockworks of the bike. The art was in the function. "I like all the nuts and bolts and fittings, the linkages and the mechanicalness of it. I like to see all the mechanicalness," he told the TV cameras.

Paul Yaffe's bike was a stretched, bright red, pro-street design called the *Phantom,* which shot 30-foot flames from its exhaust pipes. Paul figured that if Larry got up on his seat and surfed his bike, he could set him on fire with his scoot's flamethrower. At the build-off finale, held in Laconia, New Hampshire, as part of its annual Loudon Classic Bike Week, Paul Cox simulated Yaffe's flamethrower by lighting a spray can of cleaning fluid and blasting his own flames while Larry did a tire shredding burn-out. Larry was very personable, talking to everyone at the event and soliciting votes. His easy manner and old-school biker way stole the event. When the tire smoke cleared, Larry was the winner of the *Build-Off* and, like Jesse James and Billy Lane before him, a TV star was born.

At about this time, motorcycle show promoter John Green and I were working on an idea for our *Easyriders* Bike Shows that would involve many of the custom bike builders seen on the *Biker Build-Off* series. John agreed to bring several of these builders out to our shows to meet the public, sign autographs, take photos with fans, and show off their latest custom creations. We called it the *Easyriders* Centerfold Tour and featured such popular builders (as seen on the Discovery Channel) as Billy Lane, Eddie Trotta, Kim Suter, Kendall Johnson, Indian Larry, and Paul Yaffe. The shows were an enormous hit! People visiting the bike shows loved meeting and getting autographs from the bike building celebrities they had seen on the *Biker Build-Off* series.

Sometimes something happens on so-called reality TV that no one could have predicted. Something just clicks with the audience, such as the popularity of Jesse James' bad boy image; the success and stardom of the blue-collar Teutuls; and the bigger-than-life legend that grew up around bike builder, performance artist, and stunt man Indian Larry Desmedt.

In the summer of 2003 Hugh King brought Indian Larry and his crew back for another *Biker Build-Off* episode, this time against the winner of episode one, Billy Lane of Melbourne, Florida. Larry's metalflake root-beer creation was conjured straight from the heart and Billy's wild low-slung chopper was the perfect counterpart. But these two old-school bikers had nothing but respect for each other. They even hosted a party together during the Sturgis Rally to kick off the event. Billy's Choppers Inc. and Larry's Gasoline Alley put on a helluva wing-ding, and both Billy and Larry smoked the tires right off their bikes in the Full Throttle Saloon's burn-out pits.

"By the narrowest of margins," as Hugh King always said when announcing the outcome of an episode, Indian Larry was voted the winner of the contest for that *Build-Off*. True to his old-school roots, he took the microphone and told the gathered crowd, "There are no winners, there are no losers!" Then, he took a cutting tool and he and Billy cut the trophy into a dozen pieces, autographed each one, and gave them out to the crowd that surrounded them. Now *that*, as we say in the biker world, was showin' class! It was also brilliant TV. Between Billy's long dreadlocks and rock star looks and Larry's enigmatic and outrageous skin art (including his famous neck tattoos), this season finale was like a motorized sideshow circus.

In the summer of 2004, Indian Larry Desmedt was riding high on the success he had been waiting a lifetime to obtain as a bike builder. As the reigning champion of the *Biker Build-Off* TV series, he began working on his third *Build-Off* bike, this time going up against the Godfather of Choppers, Mondo Porras of Denver's Choppers out of Henderson, Nevada. Larry built his wildest chopper ever, known as the *Chain of Mystery* bike. This amazing motorcycle's frame was made out of heavy tow chain that was welded into a solid motorcycle rigid frame.

The *Chain of Mystery* chopper was finished on time in just 10 days. Larry and his crew rode with Mondo on his old-school digger-style chopper, through the lush North Carolina countryside on their way to the grand finale of the *Build-Off*. Mondo told me that the ride was the best one he ever had. "Riding handlebar to handlebar with Larry was an incredible experience," Mondo said. "It was all I could do to keep up."

TV crew and bikers arrived in Concord, North Carolina, to take part in the Liquid Steel Motorcycle Show. Event-goers poured into the show to ogle Mondo and Larry's Discovery Channel creations.

On Saturday, August 28, 2004, the spectators were voting to decide the winner of the *Build-Off* and Larry was performing daredevil stunts for the crowd outside. He rode his stunt bike through a wall of flames, and topped this off by doing some of his famous motorcycle stunts, including his signature bike surfing bit, standing up on the seat, his arms stretched out in the classic crucifix pose. But something was wrong. The bike was going too slow, no more than 30 miles per hour, and the front end began to wobble badly. Instead of leaning forward to grab the handlebars and then sitting back down in the saddle, as he might usually do, Larry fell backward off the bike and cracked his skull on the asphalt.

There was a collective gasp . . . and then silence. Everyone expected Larry to get back up. When he didn't, friends and crew ran to his side. He was airlifted to the hospital immediately. I was supposed to be at the taping of the *Build-Off* episode with Larry, but was attending a dealer meeting for a motorcycle aftermarket parts distributor named Drag Specialties. I can still hear Billy Lane's voice on the other end of my cell phone when he called me early on Sunday morning. "Larry fell off his bike and they don't know if he's gonna make it." Mondo called minutes later and gave me more details. He and Billy, as well as Larry's wife, Bambi, were all at the hospital. On Monday, August 30th, the man known as Indian Larry slipped out of this world.

Larry's death was a great shock for Hugh King and the *Build-Off* crew. They canceled airing that episode during the season and later used the footage to compile a tribute to the man whose fame went far beyond the series. Sometimes something real happens and reality TV gets *real*. From pixelating TV tubes across the country, Americans got a taste of what it was like to live outside the box, to live in the moment and be truly free . . . thanks to Indian Larry. We miss you down here, brother.

All this two-wheeled TV over the past five years has had an enormous impact on the motorcycle aftermarket industry. In just five years this industry has exploded with more parts, products, and motorcycles than at any time in the history of motorcycling. There are more people riding bikes, more riders customizing their bikes, and more information due to motorcycle magazines, television, and the Internet available to riders than ever before.

Of all the motorcycle mavericks seen on TV, Jesse James and Billy Lane stand out as rebels who fascinate both straight citizens and bikers alike. Both men have attitude and a certain edginess that makes them seem just a little dangerous. As we all know, danger is fascinating and sexy: Jesse with his Long Beach street gang looks and "Pay Up Sucker" tattoos . . . Billy with his dreadlocks and rock star persona. Watching these guys reminds me of visiting tigers at the zoo. It's safe to watch them from behind the glass, but just think what could happen if they should get out.

"I gotta hurry home—the Biker Build-Off *is coming on."*

Jesse is living the millionaire's lifestyle, free to do whatever his heart desires, from building bikes in his shop, West Coast Choppers, to kicking back at Sandra Bullock's ranch in Texas. Billy's story has panned out differently. At the height of his fame and career, having become a TV star and author of several best-selling books, Billy was involved in a traffic accident in Florida which left another man dead. He is currently going through the court system and while he is hoping for the best, he is also prepared for the worst.

The popularity of motorcycles and bike building on television instigated many Americans to think about buying motorcycles in the past five years. A large number of them did, and for a few years choppers were all the rage. This over-inflated the aftermarket industry. By 2005, every Tom, Dick, and Harry had opened a custom bike shop. Just paint a sign with any name you can think of and add the word "choppers" to the end of it. Hell, it looked easy enough on TV, right?

Well, Tom's Choppers and Dick's Choppers are already out of business and Harry is struggling. They all found out what old-school builders have known for over 30 years, namely, if bike building was easy and profitable, everyone would do it. The fact is, bike building is not an easy thing to do well. It is a craft that must be learned and honed over many years to gain the respect of your peers in the industry and the industry itself. And it's most definitely not something you do to get rich quick; you do it because you love to build choppers and don't want to do anything else. Only a lucky few builders ever earn a living doing what they love.

Ask any custom bike builder and they'll tell you that you have to have a real passion for motorcycles to make a business in fabricating work. You have to live, breathe, and eat motorcycles 24/7. Most successful builders do what they do because they love bikes, period. If they were in business strictly to make a bunch of money, they'd probably be doing something else.

Television watchers are a fickle lot and by 2006, just as quickly as they embraced bike fabrication shows, they turned away from them. Suddenly, sales of factory customs plummeted. The faucet that had been turned on so quickly when Americans wanted choppers in their garages was shut off just as quickly when everyone with the disposable income had their choppers. All of a sudden, there were factory choppers sitting in dealerships all over the country, all gathering dust and costing the dealership a monthly fee for flooring. As you might imagine, it doesn't take too many months of this before dealers go upside down on their finances. The manufacturers of these bikes, such as American IronHorse and Big Dog, had a hard time turning away from the chopper model bikes since they were geared up to produce them by the boatload. So, while the epidemic of TV shows created a lot of momentum for the motorcycle industry, it also over-inflated it.

Luckily, the dropoff in bike and parts sales leveled out and the industry resumed its normal course by the spring of 2007. The white hot fire of interest in custom choppers inspired by the Discovery Channel's bike building shows may have cooled somewhat, but the steady blaze of two-wheeled passion has resumed and continues.

While the plethora of cable TV networks turned to shows about bounty hunters and tattoo parlors as their next source of exploitation, one network that has always been dedicated to gearheads has remained steadfast in the airing of four- and two-wheeled TV. The SPEED Channel is known for showing car and bike races of all kinds, how-to shows, and the popular Barret-Jackson Auto Auctions. Custom motorcycle shows on SPEED include the long running *American Thunder*, *Corbin's Ride On*, and *V-Twin TV*. I have the honor of being the host of *V-Twin TV*, a half-hour weekly series that focuses on real bike builders building real bikes. Once the bike is built, we give it away to some lucky viewer. No one throws hammers or yells at anyone on this show. There's no race against the clock and no turning bikes into lawnmowers or making them into "theme" bikes. Just the real deal. You can catch it on Tuesday nights on SPEED. Check your local listings for dates and times, as they say in show biz land. Okay, end of shameless plug.

While Americans in the early twenty-first century were being held captive by a love for choppers, and the airwaves and magazines were primarily focused on the War in Iraq, the economy, and who would win on *American Idol*, one percenters were pretty much ignored—even when they were shooting at each other. Unlike the media explosions that made legends out of Hollister, Laconia, and Altamont, the next scene in the one percenter saga went almost unnoticed by all but the riding public.

THE LAUGHLIN SHOOTOUT

The outlaw world is never quiet. Somewhere, some one percenter motorcycle club is always at war with a rival club. This is nothing new; one percenter clubs have fought each other for turf since there have been one percenter clubs. These biker wars have ranged from street rumbles, bare-knuckle fights, and knifings in the best *West Side Story* tradition, to all-out warfare with guns and even bombings of rival clubhouses. Normally, one percenter motorcycle clubs handle their battles in private, in dark places, away from public scrutiny. But no one expected the bloodshed that took place under the bright lights of a famous gambling casino when two rival clubs suddenly went toe to toe. The little desert gaming town of Laughlin, Nevada, was ill-prepared for the shootout that occurred on Saturday, April 27, 2002.

The Mongols and the Hells Angels had been keeping an uneasy peace before 2002's annual Laughlin River Run, where over 40,000 mostly rubbie riders showed up for a weekend of gambling, partying, and riding. They never anticipated the events that unfolded. According to law enforcement intelligence, usually gathered by informants within the clubs, the gunfight occurred because the Mongols intended to bolster its status by attacking members of the Hells Angels.

Whatever the motivation, a genuine Wild West shootout took place inside Harrah's Laughlin Casino, leaving three dead and dozens wounded. According to a report in the *Las Vegas Review-Journal*, one of the dead was a Hells Angel and one was a Mongol. As stated in the arrest report, the casino had a matrix of video surveillance cameras covering the scene of the shootout and police were able to watch the tapes over and over again to try to figure out what happened. They were supposedly able to figure out who some of the shooters were and arrested one man in connection to the shooting. I have talked to insiders who have seen the tapes and some say that an undercover cop actually started the massacre by shooting first.

The violence in the casino occurred just hours after a Hells Angel was found shot to death in San Bernardino, California. Casino sources said that the HA's were hanging out at the Flamingo Hotel, got word of the shooting in Berdoo, and rode over to Harrah's to confront the Mongols. The Flamingo was traditionally Hells Angels territory during the run, as was Harrah's for the Mongols.

Casino industry sources were also quoted as saying that police warned of possible violence that weekend due to other recent battles between Southern California one percenter motorcycle clubs. Gee, no kidding. Normally, at bike runs and events, if a one percenter club shows up, the rubs just point at them and make snide comments about outlaws being losers or dinosaurs in this modern age. It reminds me of tourist-riders at the annual Sturgis Bike Rally stopping to take pictures of a herd of bison as they stroll nonchalantly across a South Dakota street. They smile and point, as if the buffaloes are just big, friendly teddy bears. But any one of those bison could get a wild hair and gore or trample those yuppies without breaking a sweat.

Once again, you can dress a sheep up like a wolf, but that doesn't make him a wolf. All the doctor and lawyer weekend warriors out there aboard their shiny new Harleys can dress up in their fancy leathers and pretend to be bad asses on the weekends, but that doesn't make them about anything. It sure as hell doesn't make them one percenters. Members of outlaw motorcycle clubs don't just ride on the weekends; the club and their bikes are their lives. Their originals are not costumes that they hang up and forget about during the work week; their colors never run.

There's an old story that a Diablo MC member told me once about a prospector who was out west during the gold rush, panning for gold. One day a rockslide came crashing down and buried a baby rattlesnake. Well, being alone all the time and kind of lonely, the prospector lifted the little snake out of the rubble and took him home to his tiny shack.

Every night, the prospector would come home, pet the little snake on the head, feed him a little sugar water, and tell him about his day. The snake slowly got better and started growing. Even when the rattler was fully grown and a beautiful specimen, the prospector would come home, pet him on the head, and talk to him before feeding him a mouse or a rabbit.

Then one day, the old prospector came home as usual, proud of the rabbit he had caught for the snake. As he reached down to pet the snake, it tagged him right on the hand. WHOMP! "Snake," the prospector cried, "you bit me and now I'm gonna die from your poison. Then I won't be able to feed you and you'll die here in this cabin. What were you thinkin'?"

The rattler just looked up at the prospector and hissed, "You knew I was a snake when you brought me in here."

The point is, a snake is always gonna be a snake, a tiger can't change his stripes or a leopard his spots, and a one percenter is a one percenter . . . a rebel to the core. By definition, a one percenter lives outside of society's laws.

CHAPTER 11

Beyond Here There Be Dragons

THE END OF THE COWBOY, THE DEATH OF THE ONE
PERCENTER. WHERE WILL THE NEXT REBELS COME
FROM? REBELLION IS BORN IN NEW, WIDE OPEN
FRONTIERS. HOW THE INTERNET WILL CREATE
THE NEXT BREED OF REBELS.

"They're the Wild Bill Hickoks, the Billy the Kids—they're the last American heroes we have, man."

—ED "BIG DADDY" ROTH, TALKING ABOUT ONE PERCENTERS

Whenever there has been a new frontier to explore, the first daring men who braved the unknown were the wild ones. Imagine what it must have been like to cast yourself into the endless ocean in a leaky ship to travel beyond all the maps in order to bring back news of exotic lands. Imagine overcoming your fear of what lay in the fog, what monsters lurked there to devour entire galleons. The wild ones were always the first to brave the strange and haunted places; they were the first in battle and the first to spit in the devil's eye. There have always been these one percenters . . . the ones who dare to go where no man has gone before.

We have seen the same drama played out time and time again. First, a bold few venture forth into the unknown to bring back wealth and discoveries. They push past the borders of reality in search of freedom, fortune, and glory. Many die in these hostile lands, but more come and soon a community is born. Unfortunately, with communities come rules. Even in the mythic pirate haven of Libertaria there were rules of conduct. Eventually, the new world becomes much like the old world and new boundaries are drawn on the map. What were once endless and uncharted seas and lands are now easily viewed in great detail on Google Earth from your home computer.

Once the wild ones do their job the bureaucrats rush in, making rules, making sure that you are safe, or at least giving you the illusion of safety to ensure their own job security. Before long, the rule makers and their police force try to eliminate the very wild ones who dared to take those first voyages into the new frontier. Look back at the Visigoths, the Huns, the Vikings, the Templars, the pirates. All pushed past the known edges of the world. Look at the American frontiersman, the mountain man, the cowboy. All reached beyond the edges of the map and drew in new lines.

In all lands and times the rebels have been those few who dared to reach beyond what was known; they were one percenters, all. In every case, once the map has been drawn and the great boundless frontier has been packaged and labeled, more people and cities follow and the wild ones are forced to move on. In the American West, wagon trains brought settlers farther and farther west. Steel tracks were soon laid from sea to shining sea and the locomotive brought men and women from many lands in search of a new way of life, new possibilities.

Just as we have seen the end of the golden age of pirates and the end of the Wild West gunslingers, so the outlaw bikers would appear from a distance to be a dying breed. Most of the original wild ones are dead and buried and many more are grandpas or great-grandpas. The RICO Act has made sure many one percenters are in prisons across the country so that Americans everywhere can have the illusion of safety.

As we have seen, today's mainstream motorcycle enthusiasts are a far cry from the one percenter. The look and feel of outlaw biker culture has been embraced by the masses, homogenized and packaged in a way that makes it acceptable to the mild ones. Thanks to humorous parodies such as the film *Wild Hogs*, we can all sit back and laugh at the craggy old one percenters as if they are lions who have been defanged and declawed for our amusement; they have been transformed into sideshow performers under the big top. It's sort of like airplane food: it looks like real food but it sure doesn't taste like it. Many rubbie riders may almost look like the real thing, but meet a true one percenter and you'll realize that a real biker is a different breed. One percenters are outsiders; they don't live by or play by the rules and they don't play well with others. They are rebels who run with scissors.

It would seem that the days of the free-spirited road rebel might be drawing to a close. However, police agencies all over the globe see it differently. To hear their statistics, they would tell you that outlaw biker motorcycle club activity is on the rise and that the specter of one percenter legions intent on world domination is imminent. According to the Bureau of Alcohol, Tobacco, Firearms, and Explosives figures, there are close to 60,000 full patch members of various one percenter clubs rampaging around the world, even in emerging countries, all poised to control drugs, prostitution, and weapons running from every cubbyhole and cranny. This seems extremely unlikely, but then paranoia drives security and defense budgets and validates these entities' existences. If the real numbers of one percenters who engage in such nefarious activities were made public, these alarmist law enforcement officials might have to go out and get real jobs.

The fact is that while overall motorcycle sales are at an all time high, with Harley-Davidson selling over 200,000 new bikes a year, the percentage of bikers who are one percenters continues to be one percent of the riding population or less.

Whether there will be one percenters riding flame painted, two-wheeled hydrogen-cell contraptions in 50 years or customized anti-gravity hover bikes in 100 years, is anyone's guess. Regardless, there will always be rebels. There will always be those brave and bold souls who dare to discover new frontiers, whether they explore outer space, other dimensions, or the bottom of the sea.

In every age, culture, and society there is a need for the rebel. It is the nonconformist who dares to ask the hard questions and push humankind forward. It has always been so, and now we need new thoughts and new ideas more than ever before. Here we spin on a ball in space, six billion plus hominids, in transit from the world that was to the world that is becoming. Our planet is an incubator, seeking new visions to embrace a new greening.

In our lifetime we will choose whether our species will continue. Because of humankind's endless expansion, animal species are becoming extinct at an alarming rate every day. In fact, the last time this planet saw so many species disappearing in such a short space of time was when the

The Laughlin Shootout was like a scene right out of the Old West.

dinosaurs disappeared. At the same time, the human population has doubled since 1960. Dr. David Ulansey, professor at the California Institute for Integral Studies, has done some startling research on what is being called the Sixth Mass Extinction. According to his research, which was published in the *New Scientist* in 2004, he believes that half of all species of life may be extinct in 50 years and that we don't have 50 years to solve this problem. Rather, we have a decade. As an example, he cites African lions, a species that has seen its population plummet by 90 percent in the past few decades. Nothing this destructive has taken place for 65 million years. Scientists predict that global warming will cause more extinction of species to occur through extreme heat, glacial melting, the rising of ocean temperatures, and water levels. Millions of humans in areas near sea level will perish or become global refugees. The hothouse this world is becoming will create more disease-carrying insects and more virulent forms of bacteria that will breed new diseases. If the earth's seas grow warmer by just a few more degrees, we will see a reversal of oceanic currents that could produce another Ice Age.

Randy Hayes, an expert in the area of environmental sustainability and founder of the Rainforest Action Network, believes that we're in a dangerous moment in history. He believes that we are shredding the fabric of the earth's life support systems, the ability of the planet to support life and future generations. According to Ulansey, Hayes, and most credible scientists, we have a very short time to turn this thing around folks. It can be done, but it will take radical thought, fierce determination, the cooperation of all nations of the world, and it will take the kind of human who dares to go beyond convention . . . it will take rebels and nonconformists. It will take the one percenter mentality to push change forward if our children and their children are to survive.

The next breed of rebels will be you and me, because we are all in this together. Perhaps some of you saw the brilliant film, *V for Vendetta*, in which a rebellious hero emerges to help the people free themselves from tyranny. The hero wears a mask. The mask is not to hide his own identity but to declare that who he is does not matter. The hero can be everyone; he is you and me. Should he fall in battle, any one of us may pick up the mask and become V. We are all in this fight together. We are all the rebel alliance.

It comes down to this: one world. We don't have another. There are no other choices. If we screw this up, our species will go the way of the dinosaur. The mask is being handed to you now. Will you pick it up?

The biker image has gone from the wild ones to the mild ones, but regular working stiffs still seek adventure on two wheels.

Lifelong biker and former editor of Easyriders, *Frank Kaisler (right) hears the story of the one that got away from bike builder Bob Abrew.*

As we have seen, the seeds of rebellion have sprouted remarkable forces that now have the power to change our lives, our societies, and our future. But in a nation of bleating sheep, we must call forth the wolves once more. It is time for the wild ones to pave the way yet again, and this time, nothing less than our survival on this planet is at stake.

Shall we sail forbidden waters? Shall we venture off the map yet again? The time has come to release the wolves and the one percenter spirit is straining at its leash.

The rebel in you is calling. Will you answer the call?

CURRENT BOOKS ABOUT ONE PERCENTER CLUBS AND INFORMANTS

In the last few years there has been a rash of books about what it's like to be on the inside with a one percenter motorcycle club. A few of these are by members of clubs such as Sonny Barger's excellent book, *Hell's Angel: The Life and Times of Sonny Barger and the Hell's Angels Motorcycle Club*. There are also books that have been written by informants (better known as rats). The following is a brief list of some of these that are worth a look. All are available through Whitehorse Press (1-800-531-1133).

Angels of Death: Inside the Biker Gangs' Crime Empire
By Julian Sher and William Marsden
This book takes readers inside the Arizona chapter of the Hells Angels and the biggest American police undercover operation to infiltrate the club. It also looks at the club's links to organized crime in Canada, Australia, Curaçao, Copenhagen, and Helsinki.

Running with the Devil: The True Story of the ATF's infiltration of the Hells Angels
By Kerrie Droban
More on the infiltration of the Arizona chapter by several cops who designed a fake Mexican motorcycle club in order to hang with the Angels. This led to a major bust in 2003 in which ATF agents arrested 50 people, seized 650 guns, 30,000 rounds of ammo, and over 100 explosive devices.

President of the Ventura, California, chapter of the Hells Angels, George Christie was born the same year the club was founded. Of the Hells Angels, he once said, "Our quest for freedom speaks for itself."

Hell's Angel: The Life and Times of Sonny Barger and the Hell's Angels Motorcycle Club

By Ralph "Sonny" Barger

Sonny describes the origins of the Hells Angels, shares memories and stories about the club's most outrageous members, and reveals the inner workings of the club—the rites, rituals, and regulations of this democratic brotherhood.

Hell's Angels Motorcycle Club

By Andrew Shaylor

The first thing you need to know about this book is that it is about a British chapter of the red and white. That said, photographer Andrew Shaylor was given full access to the club in England to go behind the scenes and capture his depiction of the club.

Hell's Angels: A Strange and Terrible Saga

By Hunter S. Thompson

I had to include this one because, though the book is dated, it's still the book that brought Hunter Thompson fame for his gonzo journalistic wit. He hangs with the Oakland chapter, goes on runs, gets his ass kicked. It's a fun, though warped, read.

Hells Angels: "Three Can Keep a Secret if Two Are Dead"

By Yves Lavigne

A collection of stories by club members as told to journalist Yves Lavigne about club life. Some are funny, some are gruesome, some are meant for shock value.

The Original Wild Ones: Tales of the Boozefighters Motorcycle Club

By Bill Hayes

Bill is a member of the Boozefighters and he tells a good tale or two here, from the events surrounding how the club came together to Hollister, to *The Wild One* and beyond. This is a good read and you get the feeling of what it must have been like to ride with Wino Willie Forkner.

Under and Alone: The True Story of the Undercover Agent Who Infiltrated America's Most Violent Outlaw Motorcycle Gang

By William Queen

I both love and hate this book. On the plus side it is a well-written book about ATF agent William Queen infiltrating the San Fernando chapter of the Mongols Motorcycle Club. He lives the part of a one percenter, gets inside, becomes a member, and gets confused because he has to bust men that have truly become his brothers. On the negative side, the dude's a rat.

A Wayward Angel: The Full Story of the Hells Angels by the Former Vice President of the Oakland Chapter

By George Wethern

This book is billed as a brutal inside account of the Hells Angels as told by one of the club's most notorious leaders. If that is what you want, read Sonny's book and get the real deal.

INDEX